The
PEASENHALL
MURDER

The PEASENHALL MURDER

An Edwardian Mystery

NEIL NORMAN

PEN & SWORD
TRUE CRIME

First published in Great Britain in 2024 by
PEN AND SWORD TRUE CRIME
An imprint of
Pen & Sword Books Ltd
Yorkshire – Philadelphia

ISBN 978 1 39906 437 8

Typeset in Times New Roman 12/17 by SJmagic DESIGN SERVICES, India.
Printed and bound in the UK by CPI Group (UK) Ltd, Croydon, CR0 4YY.

Pen & Sword Books Limited incorporates the imprints of Atlas, Archaeology,
Aviation, Discovery, Family History, Fiction, History, Maritime, Military,
Military Classics, Politics, Select, Transport, True Crime, Air World, Frontline
Publishing, Leo Cooper, Remember When, Seaforth Publishing, The Praetorian
Press, Wharncliffe Local History, Wharncliffe Transport, Wharncliffe True Crime
and White Owl.

For a complete list of Pen & Sword titles please contact
PEN & SWORD BOOKS LIMITED
George House, Units 12 & 13, Beevor Street, Off Pontefract Road,
Barnsley, South Yorkshire, S71 1HN, England
E-mail: enquiries@pen-and-sword.co.uk
Website: www.pen-and-sword.co.uk

or

PEN AND SWORD BOOKS
1950 Lawrence Rd, Havertown, PA 19083, USA
E-mail: uspen-and-sword@casematepublishers.com
Website: www.penandswordbooks.com

Contents

Contents

Introduction

There is a great fascination regarding unsolved murder that far outweighs any case that is solved. Just ask any person in the street about great unsolved murders in the United Kingdom and the odds are high that the first name they will say would be that of Jack the Ripper. Of course, this is a pseudonym because the mystery of his identity following his autumn reign of terror is still very much alive, 134 years later. This is but one example of many crimes across the nation which have occurred where no culprit has been brought to justice – or perhaps a suspect has been placed on trial only for a set of circumstances to see the accused walk free.

The Peasenhall murder of 1902 is one such case that grabbed the nation's attention, only for it to reach a most unsatisfactory conclusion that left both the family of victim Rose Anne Harsent, and the general public alike, without closure.

As we shall see, the Peasenhall case looked, on paper, to be a judicial formality only for the case to be thrown into complete chaos on two separate occasions, which resulted in this case remaining in the annals of unsolved crimes of the United Kingdom.

Peasenhall is a village that lies within the agricultural county of Suffolk on the eastern side of England. It is an idyllic place where old country lanes weave their way through the landscape and hedgerows align the streets. The village is situated some 22 miles from Lowestoft. The village was built with the knowledge and skills of generations of craftsmen trained mainly in agriculture and is a place where people could easily thrive from the rich-fertile soil.

In the early part of the nineteenth century there were three blacksmiths, three shoemakers and three wheelwrights, not to mention a saddle, collar maker, a cooper, bricklayer, two carpenters, a plumber and glazier. There was also a corn merchant and the Smyth family, who operated a business of making seed and manure drills. A hive of activity, the tiny village of Peasenhall, with its constant inhabitant rate of between 700-800 people would fit seamlessly in any story written by Sir Arthur Conan Doyle for his master of sleuthing, Sherlock Holmes.

Chapter One

The Respectably Married Man and the Servant Girl

William Gardiner was, at the time of the murder, a highly thought of and respected member of the community within Peasenhall. He was the foreman carpenter of Smyth's Seed Drill Works, as well as the Sibton Chapel class leader, Sunday School Superintendent, Society Steward and organist. These were all positions he had attained by his strong character and dedicated hard work; all very much surprising given that he was born on 22 December 1866 at Blything Parish Union Workhouse at Bulcamp.

William's mother, Caroline Gardiner, was born in 1845 and lived with her mother, father and five siblings in Great Street in Yoxford before moving, ten years later, to Brook Street, also within the village. At nineteen she became pregnant and on 2 November 1864, she gave birth to a daughter, Anna Maria Gardiner, at the Bulcamp Workhouse. Anna was followed by the birth of her next sibling, William George Gardiner, on 22 December 1866 and, finally, Caroline gave birth to her third child, Ada Jane Gardiner, on 28 May 1869. All three were born at the workhouse.

Caroline was, by profession, a housemaid and, being unmarried, she would have lost her job with each resulting pregnancy as soon as it became apparent that she was with child. This of course would have serious financial repercussions for young Caroline because the fees needed for the midwife and doctor during the pregnancy could only be obtained if she declared herself without means and then declared herself to the workhouse which had an on-site hospital. Once a child was born she would then leave the workhouse and move to her parents' house before trying to find employment again or, more likely, become pregnant again, and begin the cycle anew. In 1873, she married Edward Coleman, a shoemaker, and her life became stable but the tarnish to her pride had already been cast.

From such a difficult start in life, it appears that Gardiner received a good education at Yoxford parish school and in 1881, aged just fourteen, he left school and began working as an apprentice wheelwright, making and repairing wheels for carts and so on, a job which requires great attention to detail and precise measurements.

In 1888 he became a qualified wheelwright and it was on 16 October that year he married Georgianna Cady at Westleton Primitive Methodist Chapel. It is interesting to note that Georgianna was already seven months pregnant at this time, so perhaps it was a wedding somewhat forced upon the couple by the bride's father, George Cady. Additional support to this theory lies on the wedding certificate, on which William stated he lived in a place called Elmswell, some thirty-five miles from Yoxford. The true reason will never be known, but we do know that the couple very shortly returned to Yoxford after the wedding and, in December of that year, they welcomed their first child into the world, Ettie May Gardiner, who was born at her grandparents' house there.

Georgianna was one of seven children born to George Cady and his wife. Georgianna was born in 1868 in the family home in Great Street, Yoxford, a village located just two miles from Peasenhall. This was to be the place of her upbringing where her father, George Cady, ran the local grocery store. Georgianna was schooled within the village and upon leaving would take up the role of apprentice dressmaker before she was to fall pregnant in 1888.

Cady was also a preacher at the local Primitive Methodist Connexion and it's clear by his later positions within the church that Gardiner wanted to reach the heights his father-in-law had attained.

Within a couple of years, Gardiner, his wife and daughter moved the short distance of four miles to Peasenhall, where he found employment as a carpenter for the local undertaker, Newberry. This was a local tried and tested way to eventually gain employment at Smyth's Seed Drill and Works; the biggest and highest paying employer within the area. It wasn't long before an opportunity became available there and he took the position of wheelwright and carpenter where he gained a reputation for meticulous and hard work.

It was also around this time that Gardiner began his rise within the Primitive Methodist Church, a major offshoot of the Methodist religion that was popular in Victorian and Edwardian times. In an ironic twist, his father-in-law, George Cady, who was a preacher and well established member, resigned in early 1892 due to bankruptcy. This gave Gardiner the perfect excuse to execute his plan to rise within the ranks of the church at his father-in-law's expense. In just four years at his workplace – between 1898 and 1901 – he went from wheelwright, to foreman carpenter, to outside manager with his own office beside that of his boss, Mr Smyth. He was even sent to the Paris Exhibition in 1900 to supervise their trade stand there.

Between 1891 and 1901 his family also grew: Ida Mildrid was born in 1891 and Ernest William followed quickly in 1892. There was then a four year gap before any more children arrived, in which it is believed that Georgianna suffered one or more miscarriages, but in 1896, Bertie George was born and was followed two years later by twin daughters Annie and Dora in 1898 and finally, in 1901, came Daisy May.

One can argue at this point that Gardiner had an almost perfect life – a devoted family man, highly respected in both workplace and place of worship – but something was obviously not quite right in his mind because he would soon show a wandering eye towards a young servant girl, Rose, who lived with her employers at Providence House, the large house just down the road from his humble cottage.

Rose Anne Harsent was born in March 1879 in Sibton and was the fourth of nine children born to her parents William and Elizabeth. Her education was conducted at Sibton Parish School though it appears she was absent more than she was in attendance.

Her association with the Primitive Methodist Church began as a teenager in 1898 and her interest no doubt started due to a young man called Bob Kerridge, a local ploughboy and regular at the church, with whom she struck up a friendship. By 1900 they were engaged, although this seems to have been more of a mutual agreement, as Rose was never seen to wear a ring that confirmed the arrangement between the two, but Rose's mother did certainly believe that they would one day be married.

Rose loved music and the church gave her the opportunity to sing in the choir; she quickly wanted to learn to play the organ too and it was to be Kerridge who would buy her a small harmonium, which was a popular form of evening entertainment in homes of the time.

It is fair to say that Rose was an average-looking girl, but it is in little doubt that she was a bubbly and popular girl around the village and she was admired by several young men, one of whom was Frederick Davis, who was four years her junior and worked as a grocer's boy at the local Emmett's store. Through his job, which included delivering groceries to Providence House, he often saw Rose and soon got to know her. He was also a weekly attendee of the Sibton Chapel and their friendship grew strong.

Davis was a keen writer, not in the sense of poetic verse but more in the way of a racier type of poem and verse, which it appears Rose was rather fond of. He wrote her conventional love letters in which he left nothing to the imagination in his desire for Rose and he would even quote the more passionate verses of the Bible. Though his constant and unrelenting attempts of trying to become physically involved with Rose were evident, there is no evidence that he had achieved his dreams with her at any point of their friendship. It is, of course, often the case when romantic aspirations are dealt a heavy blow that 'jilted lovers' can become violent and aggressive in their rejection, and so it seems odd that Davis was never looked at as a real suspect of Rose's murder, even when, later in the investigation, his letters to her were found.

Rose began work at Providence House in 1900 and was employed by Mr and Mrs Crisp. William Crisp was a retired tailor and also an elder at the Doctor's Chapel, (a small building built in 1684 as a place to deliver congregational lectures weekly) and Georgiana Crisp was, by all accounts, a rather eccentric lady of a nervous disposition. They employed Rose as a domestic servant girl at the house, whose duties also involved cleaning the chapel one evening a week. Rose worked hard and there is no doubt that she had good working and personal relationships with her employers, but within eighteen months of her initial employment everything would be thrown into turmoil.

Chapter Two

A Village Scandal is Born

Wednesday, 1 May 1901, was a typically warm late Spring day in Peasenhall, yet this day, which had began as unassuming as any other, was to be the beginning of a chain of events that would ultimately lead to murder some twelve months later.

On this day, William Gardiner was out of town on work that would eventually see him return home at 7.30 in the evening. He had been out driving the Works' cart that, on this occasion, was being pulled by a different horse than that which he was accustomed to – a stallion rather than his faithful black mare. At the Works he fed and watered the horse before rubbing it down. The horse didn't take up its food, which worried Gardiner because he was responsible for the care of the horses in the yard. With this playing on his mind, he walked home for tea which he usually had at 6.00 each evening; he was already nearly two hours late. On his journey home, Gardiner met Bill Wright in Rendham Road; Wright was a 20-year-old wheelwright at Smyths' under the charge of Gardiner. They exchanged pleasantries before Gardiner made his way home to eat and as soon as he finished he told his wife that he had to go back to the horse to see if it had eaten up and if not, he would call for the vet. On his way back up Rendham Road, Gardiner again encountered Wright, though this time they didn't speak. Gardiner then approached the stables at the Works and discovered that the horse had eaten and was well. After finishing up he began to make his way home. Not far into the lane he heard Rose Harsent calling out to him from across the way, which was a barred gated narrow path that led up to the Doctor's Chapel, where she had just cleaned. She claimed that the door was sticking and that she could not lock it and so Gardiner walked back with Rose to the chapel to inspect the door, finding that the wood was swollen from earlier rain, and that he had to slam it shut with some considerable force. They then spent a short time discussing the hymns that were to be sung during the chapel's impending anniversary before walking together until separating at the crossroads to go to their individual homes. This was the official version of events that would later be given by Gardiner but the events were to be told differently by Bill Wright, who had a witness to back him up.

Wright said that between 7.30 and 7.45pm, he was walking down Rendham Hill. He had observed Rose coming down the hill also and turning into the alley that led up to the Doctor's Chapel. He thought no more of this and continued on his way until he met Gardiner coming up the hill. They briefly spoke, as suggested in Gardiner's story of events. Wright obviously had little else to do because he spent some time loitering around the area and saw Gardiner coming back down the hill some five minutes later, appearing to be headed towards his home.

Being a typical warm, mid-week evening, Wright continued to hang around the area, just kicking his heels, no doubt. Between 8.00 and 8.15pm he once again saw Gardiner walking up Rendham Hill. Unlike in Gardiner's account, Wright claimed that Gardiner did in fact speak to him on this second occasion, asking Wright how long he'd kept his dog and also saying that it looked like they were due some rain. Wright then watched Gardiner make his way up the hill until he turned into the alley that led to the Doctor's Chapel.

Wright must have been overcome with curiosity; perhaps sensing that something was about to happen, he wasted no time and ran to his stepfather's cottage on the corner of Hackney Road, where he shared a room with Alfonso Skinner who Wright thought would also be interested in his news. Skinner was a 26-year-old fitter at the Drill Works and though Gardiner wasn't his direct boss, any inclination of potential gossip would be too much to resist.

Both Wright and Skinner approached the Doctor's Chapel at around 8.20pm. They positioned themselves behind a fence at the back of the south-west window and there they remained for over an hour. There was no light inside the chapel but for candles as dusk fell, but a crescent moon was providing the light they needed. At first the young men heard talking and laughter, followed by rustling and the sound of the thin-paned glass window shaking. A female voice was heard to say 'OH! OH!' and the voice was instantly recognized by Wright to belong to Rose. He then said he heard more noise, which he interpreted as the pair putting their clothes back on. At this point Wright, for some reason, left the scene, leaving Skinner to hear the best bit of the chapel encounter. The female voice was heard to say, 'Did you notice me reading my Bible last Sunday?'

'What were you reading'?' asked Gardiner.

'I was reading about like what we have been doing here tonight, I'll tell you where it is. Thirty-eighth chapter of Genesis.'

There can be no doubt as to what they were referring to; a look at the verse will leave the reader in little doubt too:

> And Onan knew that the seed should not be his, and it came to
> pass, when he went in unto his brother's wife, that he spilled
> it on the ground, lest that he should give seed to his brother.

It should be noted that the Victorians used the term 'Onanism' to describe the act of masturbation, and the fact that Rose should mention this can surely mean that the act was performed within the Chapel that evening.

She was heard to also say, 'it won't be noticed'. Shortly after this Wright came back and the two men stayed a further fifteen minutes before hearing the woman say, 'You must let me go'. Skinner also heard her say, 'I shall be out tomorrow night at 9 o'clock.' It was at this time both Wright and Skinner decided to leave. Wright made haste in his getaway but Skinner was more casual in his retreat from the scene and he witnessed Rose leave the chapel and run down Rendham Road towards her residence, Providence House. Skinner noted that Gardiner was much more cautious when leaving the chapel and, once Rose was out of sight, he picked up his pace and Skinner joined him for the last part of the journey. At the crossroads they parted; Skinner turned left to go home, but noticed Gardiner crossed straight across the road, towards Mill Lane, instead of turning right along the street where his cottage was located. Gardiner was to meet Wright once more that night, when he appeared to have asked Wright once more about his dog. Wright replied that his dog was deceased. Wright and Skinner now held in their possession gossip that they would reveal to their fellow villagers, and so began the scandal that would rock not just the local community but later go on to make national news. With the differing accounts given here by Gardiner, Wright and Skinner, it is of note that none of the men wavered in their recount of events.

Wright and Skinner's sensational news spread like wildfire. A highly respected man of the community in both work and chapel duties, not to mention a married man with six children, being involved with a servant girl thirteen years his junior was a major event in such a tiny village. Unsurprisingly, it was within the week when Gardiner heard of the whisperings going on around him about his conduct that evening with Rose at the Doctor's Chapel. Gardiner decided to not inform his wife as she had just given birth to their daughter just two days after the 'event', but to write a letter to Rose instead, informing her of the gossip that was circulating. He wrote his letter from his office and placed it within a blue envelope before handing it to Harry Harsent, Rose's brother, to take to his older sister.

He wrote as follows:

Dear Rose,
I was very much surprised this morning to hear that there's some scandal going the round about you and me going into

the Doctor's Chapel for immoral purposes so that I shall put it into other hands at once as i have found out who it was that started it. Bill Wright and Skinner say they saw us there but I shall summons them for defamation of character unless they withdraw what they have said and give me a written apology. I shall see Bob tonight and we will come and see you together if possible. I shall at some time see your father and tell him. [sic]

Yours, & C.,

William Gardiner.

Strong words indeed. The letter clearly sets out what Gardiner's intentions were, but whether or not he ever spoke to the Harsents or Bob (Kerridge), Rose's fiance, was never documented.

Gardiner was understandably under great stress now that his secret was public but things were to take another turn when his recently born daughter, Daisy May Gardiner, was to die on 2 June 1901, having been ill since she was born.

Wright and Skinner were called to Gardiner's office on 8 May. At this meeting William relayed the version of events that he had heard and asked why they should be the ones to instigate such slander. The pair responded that they were telling no lies, what they had heard and seen was nothing more than the truth. Skinner later said that Gardiner had even, at one point, denied being at the chapel that evening at all. Growing more and more frustrated with the reluctance of Wright and Skinner to recant their claims, Gardiner stepped up his intimidation of the two gentlemen, demanding an apology from them both. If they didn't agree, he would sue them both for defamation of character. Amazingly, both men were not intimidated by Gardiner's threat and stated they would not apologise because they were the ones speaking the truth. With this, the meeting ended with great ill will amongst both parties. One can only imagine the thoughts racing around in Gardiner's head. After some contemplation he decided to write to Rose again:

Dear Rose,

I have broke the news to Mrs Gardiner this morning, she is awfully upset but she say she knows it is wrong, for I was at home from half past eight till after nine and home again by nine thirty so I could not possibly be with you an hour so she won't believe anything about it. I have asked Mr Burgess to ask those too [sic] chaps to come to Chapel tonight and have it out there however they stand by such a tale I don't know but I don't think god will forsake me now and if we put our trust in him it will end right but it's awfully hard work to have to face people when they are all suspicious of you but by god's help whether they believe me or not I shall try and live it down and prove by my future conduct that it's all false, I only wish I could take it to court but I don't see a shadow of a chance to get the case as I don't think you would be strong enough to face trial. Trusting that god will direct us and make the way clear – I remain, yours in trouble.

W. Gardiner.

Gardiner's letter shows that he had reassured his wife and that she had believed him when he said that it was all a tissue of lies coming from Wright and Skinner. However, we must remember that those two men had nothing to lie about: neither had any previous issues with Gardiner, so why would he write a letter in such a manner to Rose? Other questions would be just what relationship did these letters imply? Would they have known each other well through church? Would no one question an acquaintance between them? Why didn't he write to her family to protest his fears and innocence? Could this have been an early sign of Gardiner's forward thinking? Did he possibly intend this note to be one day seen by another and absolve him of all guilt? Whatever the reason, Gardiner would now have to face an inquest at Sibton Chapel regarding the allegations and the church elders were keen to resolve this issue at the quickest convenience.

After all, the allegations made by both Wright and Skinner could throw this rural church into disarray with such a scandal. Gardiner was a pillar of society and if, in the eyes of the community, he could succumb to temptation, what hope had anyone else of keeping on the righteous path?

The inquest began on 11 May 1901. Gardiner's friend, Henry Rouse, had written to the Reverend John Guy, the Superintendent Minister of the Wangford circuit, asking for him to attend the meeting as he was the most prominent member of the chapel who could oversee the matter. Mr Guy was a middle-aged man in his fifties from Berkshire and he was charged with the duty to travel to Peasenhall. The church was not accustomed to having to respond to such requests, but this was a scandal that it could not allow to go unresolved because news spread like wildfire from village to village and town to town. Such a blemish could not be allowed to taint the reputation of the Methodists in their competition for believers of other, older, established religious organisations and so, at Rouse's request, Reverend Guy interviewed Rose whilst in the presence of her mother about the allegations made against her and Gardiner. It is clear that Guy was going through the motions because he made little effort to delve deep into the claims and was in no doubt convinced that this matter should be resolved as quickly as possible.

The inquest itself was held in the presence of twenty members of the congregation; one notable absentee was Rose herself. The meeting was long and thorough, it began between 7.00 and 7.30pm and neither Wright nor Skinner were allowed to leave until 10pm. The meeting concluded at 10.30pm and it was settled in Gardiner's favour. This wasn't surprising as Gardiner had delivered his story with strength and vigour. He denied any wrongdoing, as Rose had previously done in her meeting with Reverend Guy, whilst Wright and Skinner maintained their story. The fact that the meeting had taken some three hours does, however, show that it wasn't a straightforward formality; it did essentially sit as a 50/50 story since it was merely the word of one party against another but in the end the elders of the church were highly unlikely to turn their back on one of their own.

The fact that neither Wright or Skinner were chapel members could not have aided their cause and so, with this fact and the lack of evidence, it would only make sense that their claims would be dismissed. Despite his being found innocent, it seems rather strange that Gardiner resigned from all his duties within the chapel after the inquest. The posts he left were that of class leader, society steward, Sunday school superintendent and organist – ironically, it appears Rose was to become the organist in Gardiner's absence. As previously promised by Gardiner to Rose in his first letter, he contacted a solicitor, Mr Harold Mullens of Halesworth, to gain an apology from both Wright and Skinner for defamation of character against Gardiner. This must have been, in Gardiner's eyes, a foolproof way to show his innocence to the church, the community and his wife.

In English law a defamation of character claim would need to be proven in each of the following ways:

- A defamatory statement was made;
- The statement caused, or is likely to cause, 'serious harm' to the claimant;
- The statement refers to the claimant;
- The statement was published;
- There is no lawful justification or other defence..

According to Gardiner's thinking, he had Wright and Skinner for four of these points and so would have a strong case to have his name officially and legally cleared. But exactly what did Wright and Skinner stand to lose should Gardener win his case? The answer is nothing more than having to make an obvious and very public apology and also pay a fine to the claimant.

As the accusations were spoken this would literally have been a 'their word against mine' case and Gardener, with such a large family, no doubt couldn't afford to pursue the legal avenue considering that the financial reward would be low and he would most likely have to spend out more than he would gain; the only reward he needed was an admission of the fabrication of the truth and this was not to be forthcoming from either Wright or Skinner.

Though the church had cleared Gardiner of any wrong-doing, and despite the financial implications, Gardiner needed legal clarification to make the claims go away once and for all. He sought the help of Harold A. Mullens, a lawyer, who proceeded to send out a letter to both Wright and Skinner which reads as follows:

Sir,

Mr William George Gardiner of Peasenhall has consulted me in reference to certain slanderous statements which he alleges you have uttered and circulated concerning him and a young woman. I have to inform you that unless you tender my client an ample written apology within seven days from this date legal process will be forthwith commenced against you without further notice to yourself.

Yours faithfully
Harold A. Mullens.

It can be assumed that Reverend Guy did fully believe in Gardiner's innocence as it was noted on 26 May that whilst walking home from Wangford to his home in Halesworth (a seven mile trip) he was joined by a Mr Abraham Goddard, a farmer by trade but also a highly regarded local preacher, and a Mr William Tripp, an insurance agent and another local preacher. They discussed the situation at length and both Goddard and Tripp were convinced that Guy was fully of the opinion that Gardiner had done no wrong.

The decision was made on that evening but it was to be a month later on 26 June, at the quarterly meeting held at the chapel, where Mr Guy would give an oral report on the inquiry. He said there was nothing to the tale and that Gardiner should keep all his roles, though several were due to end at the end of the year anyway.

The letters from Mullens were received by Wright and Skinner but still they would not budge. They remained defiant, saying they had done no wrong and had just said what they had heard and seen. Gardiner was now in a position that, if he pursued the matter further, it would be at great cost to him and neither Wright or Skinner possessed anything that would be of use to him should he be successful in his prosecution, so he decided to drop all proceedings. Upon hearing of Gardiner's decision to drop all legal proceedings to prove his innocence, Mr Guy had warned him to stay away from Rose at any cost so as not to fuel any future speculation of an affair but it should also be noted that now that Gardiner was ceasing the legal aspect of his defence, it all began to look suspicious to Mr Guy, who started to think that maybe there had truly been more to this than met the eye and Gardiner, with his smooth talking, had indeed pulled the wool over Mr Guy's eyes.

So, what can be determined from the statements given so far? To a casual observer this seems like a trivial matter; a piece of gossip that should have probably circulated amongst the population before dying out after a month or so, before another event would take their interest.

The problem was that Gardiner was not prepared to let it go and have the gossip run its course, he was determined to pursue the event and get full apologies from Wright and Skinner. Given that the church had found him innocent, and his wife too had also believed him, why did he feel the need to push the matter? He must have been very confident that he would get his way, by firstly speaking with both the men and then stepping up his intimidation with legal threats. It must also be remembered that both Wright and Skinner worked at the drill works and Wright was directly under Gardiner's charge, but still they would not sway from their statements. At the inquest, both Wright and Skinner relayed the same story even though they were placed in the chapel environment, a group that they didn't belong to, surrounded by people who certainly didn't want scandal to befall their church, and it is safe to say that they both would have been subjected to great scrutiny from the church elders. The only alternative is that Wright and Skinner's version of events was the correct version. The pair had no reason to lie as this would have placed them in great jeopardy with their boss and also make them focal points of scrutiny within the community. Rose and Gardiner had indeed been at the Doctor's Chapel that night and the rumoured liaison had occurred. Gardiner was a desperate man now. He was a highly thought of employee at Smyths'; he'd been to the exhibition in France in 1900 to represent the company. He held several positions within the Methodist Church community – a man of god, and men of god should not behave this way. Finally, and perhaps most importantly, from a moral stance, Gardiner was a married man with six children. He was certainly in a position where he had little to gain and everything to lose.

Chapter Three

A Grisly Murder

Saturday, 31 May 1902 was a hot and still day and, as with many days at this time of year, thunderstorms are never far away and this night was to see a tempest of great rage pass over the village; a storm of such violence that it would remain in people's memories for many a year to come. The population of Peasenhall awaited the storm with trepidation as the clouds began to gather that evening on the horizon. The previous evening had seen a storm pass over that had caused a deluge of rain that had filled the brook that ran alongside the street, to the point of it overflowing and flooding the road. Many of the 700 or so inhabitants were watching from their doorways as the first flashes and rumbles of thunder began at 10pm.

One resident was William Gardiner, a stocky 35-year-old with jet black hair, moustache and beard. He watched the storm as it gathered in ferocity, even stepping outside his doorway at one point, whereupon he encountered Harry Burgess, a bricklayer by trade who was out on his way to Mrs Pepper's shop on the north side of the street to buy something before the rains made the journey impassable for him because he lived on the causeway, which was a line of houses that faced the brook on the southside with just a small bridge to cross which would quickly be under water. Burgess and Gardiner knew each other well, as they both attended the primitive methodist chapel at Sibton, a four-minute walk from Peasenhall. Burgess would later say that they spoke for fifteen minutes, mostly about the weather and business, before parting ways. As Burgess began to walk away he glanced over his shoulder and saw that the attic window at the top of Providence House had a candle in the window. This was Rose Harsent's room window, a servant of the house, and he thought nothing of it as her window was usually illuminated at this time of night. At the same time, Mrs Dickinson, a recent widow who was running her late husband's ironmongers shop and scared of thunder, was growing anxious as the storm began to rage overheard at 11pm. It was at this time that Mrs Georgianna Gardiner made her way to Mrs Dickinson's house to sit with her as she had made a promise to be with her in the event of a traumatic event like this storm. Mr Gardiner stayed at home for a while to make sure the Gardiner's six children were soundly asleep before walking to Mrs Dickinson's house to join his wife in keeping the widow company; a journey that he made in, it is interesting to note, a pair of carpet slippers, hardly appropriate footwear for a storm of this nature. The couple stayed until 1.30am when the worst of the storm had passed over.

At Providence House, both William and Georgiana Crisp had gone to bed at around 10.15pm that evening, about an hour before the storm had gathered its full rage. Georgiana woke that night twice; the first occasion was shortly after the storm began and she went to the bedroom window to make sure the heavy rains were not coming in. She subsequently went downstairs and closed the door between the dining room and kitchen, after checking that the rain water wasn't coming in through the back door either. She then returned to bed where some time later she was awoken again, this time by the sound of a scream, followed by a thud. Upon hearing the scream and thud, Mrs Crisp woke her husband and asked him if they should go and see if Rose was all right. He believed there was no need for this because they had previously given Rose permission to enter their bedroom should she ever become frightened of such events. With this, the couple fell back to sleep. Mrs Crisp would later say that she estimated the time of this event as being between 1.00 and 2.00am.

In the morning the storm had passed and barely any signs could be seen, but the heavy rains had left their mark. At 8.00am Rose's father, William, approached Providence House carrying Rose's clean linen as he always did every Sunday morning. He went to the back of the house, where a small conservatory surrounded the kitchen window and door. He saw that the door to the conservatory was slightly opened, something that was unusual, as was the fact that a woollen shawl was held up by a fork against the window of the conservatory. He went inside and opened the kitchen door where, to his horror, he saw his daughter lying on the floor. Rose was laying on her back with her right arm outstretched and her head against the steps that led to her attic bedroom. She was also laying in a pool of blood that spread from her head to her left on the floor, so much blood, in fact, that Mr Harsent believed he must have trodden in it, though no signs of this were subsequently found. Her throat had been cut and a bodged attempt had been made to burn the body. Her nightgown was burnt away on the sides, with the fire having burned with greater ferocity on her right side, as could be seen on her right arm and on the right side of her abdomen where her flesh was blackened. A folded copy of the local paper, *The East Anglia Daily Times*, was under her head and exhibited burning around the edges. Of interest here is that the paper was dated Friday, 30 May, one day before the murder was assumed to have taken place, and also that the Crisp family did not take this paper. The fire around her head had evidently been extinguished quickly too because there were no traces of burning to her face or hair.

Close to Rose's head lay a burnt out candlestick that she had used on what was to be her final journey that night. A paraffin oil lamp heavily coated in blood was next to the candlestick. The well of this lamp was still three-quarters full but the glass chimney was intact. The door that led to the upstairs from the kitchen was opened fully and upon it were blood splatters and smears of blood, and blood was also on the bottom two steps. Near the candlestick could be seen crushed glass and a strong smell of paraffin was very evident. This was from a medicine bottle that had been broken, with the neck of the bottle having rolled past the kitchen table, still with its cork firmly wedged inside so tightly that it could not be extracted. The glass had a pungent smell of paraffin and, for the time being, the label of the bottle was unreadable due to it being smeared with blood. Mr Harsent went over to his daughter's lifeless body and took hold of her arm; it was stone cold. It was then he saw the large slash mark across her throat which had ended her life. With this he covered her body, left Providence House and made the short journey two doors away to Mr James Crisp's house, the brother of William Crisp. Mr Harsent told him of the terrible scene that had met him as he entered Providence House before both men went back to Rose's body and more help was sent for. Mr Harsent went up the stairs to see the Crisps at around 8.45am to inform them that his daughter lay deceased in their kitchen. Mr Crisp came downstairs briefly to see the scene but Mrs Crisp would not venture down until poor Rose's body had been removed that evening.

Just across the road lived Dr Lay, the village's resident doctor, and he was summoned at 8.40am. Rose was already in a state of rigor mortis by this time and Dr Lay estimated the time of death had occurred some four to six hours earlier. His initial conclusion upon entering the kitchen and smelling the paraffin was that Rose had burned to death after falling down the stairs and hitting her head which caused her to lose consciousness at which point the paraffin had leaked onto her nightdress before catching fire in an accident with the lamp, but after closer inspection, he noted that the burns on her right side and arms showed her flesh was not blistered but charred, and this meant that she was already dead before the flames had licked her stricken body. Noting the vast amount of blood that surrounded the body and the deep gashes in her throat, a closer inspection uncovered a deep cut that ran from the left jaw all the way across to the right jaw and he determined that the cut across her left jugular vein had resulted in the extensive loss of blood that eventually had killed her. Rose's windpipe had been severed also, something else that would have caused her death. Along with these mortal injuries, several stab wounds had been delivered to the breastbone and left clavicle that then went up the left-hand side of her neck. Oddly enough however the doctor initially believed that Rose had inflicted these wounds with the intention to commit suicide, which is a bizarre conclusion indeed. After all, wouldn't it make more sense that if she was in such a despairing state she would have ended her life in the solitude of her bedroom and not in full view in the kitchen in the middle of the night. This conclusion implies that Dr Lay must have strangely deduced that the wounds were caused by Rose using an upward thrusting motion before she then attempted to slash her own throat from left to right but ran off path and stopped at her chin, before attempting the same procedure and succeeding on the second attempt with a clean cut from left to right, made with such force that it severed her windpipe. This then caused Rose to drop the lamp which started the fire, but how the neatly folded copy of *The East Anglian Daily Times* should have ended up under her head was not explained!

More evidence of foul play came in the form of a bruise on her right cheek and cuts on her hands, as well as cuts on her right forefinger, left thumb, left forefinger and ball of her left thumb. These were the wounds that perplexed the doctor as he could not easily explain them away in his theory of suicide. The local police constable, Eli Nunn, was informed of the death at Providence House and raced immediately to the scene. After he arrived he made precise notes of the surroundings in the kitchen before he and Dr Lay went up to Rose's room to look for further evidence. Upon entering the room, a brief search uncovered a letter which was inside an envelope placed on a box beside her unslept-in bed, the envelope had a Yoxford postmark on it and the letter – unsigned – within read as follows:

> D R
> I will try to see you tonight at 12 o'clock at your place if you
> put a light in your window at 10 o'clock for about 10 minutes
> then you can take it out again. Don't have a light in your room
> at 12 as i will come round to the back.

Another batch of letters were found in a chest of drawers but were of no relevance, just letters from a few local men that were of a more amorous nature or saucy postcard type of humour and some family letters. The two previous letters from William Gardiner dated the previous year were found where he had written of his intention to clear their names of the scandal that was being spread around the village. George Andrews, a superintendent from Halesworth, was called for immediately and, upon arriving at Providence House, found that Dr Lay, who was still on scene, had found a broken bottle with his handwriting on the label. The label, smeared in blood and soaked with paraffin, read 'A sixth part to be taken every four hours'. The name of the patient was unfortunately masked by the blood. Dr Lay initially believed the medicine had been prescribed for Mrs Gardiner but after the bottle had been received by a Home Office specialist on 9 June and treated to allow the label to be read, it revealed, 'two or three teaspoonfuls' and 'Mrs Gardiner's choln'. The bottle had originally contained an elixir to treat the children of a cold. But why was a medicine bottle prescribed for a family who supposedly had nothing to do with Rose or Providence House found at the scene of a murder? More interesting still, why had the original contents been replaced with paraffin?

A post-mortem was performed by Dr Lay who also acquired the services of Dr Ryder Richardson of Saxmundham to assist him. Dr Richardson quickly concluded that Rose had been murdered and that there could be no way that the wounds inflicted were resultant of a suicide. It was also quickly discovered that Rose had been six months pregnant. This now opened a can of worms…. Was this a motive for the murder? And what did the police have to go on?

The answer was the police had in their possession two letters from William Gardiner that Rose had kept from the year before that had attempted to enlighten Rose to the impending slurs upon their names. They also had a broken medicine bottle that was prescribed to the Gardiners' children placed at the murder scene and they also had a deceased 23-year-old pregnant servant girl. Clearly the first port of call of suspects to interview should be Willam Gardiner.

Chapter Four

The Investigation and Inquiry

On 3 June, William Gardiner was arrested for the murder of Rose Harsent. The truth is the arrest would surely have been made earlier had it not been for Dr Lay's original conclusion that Rose had committed suicide. The police had only circumstantial evidence and one feels that Superintendent Andrews and PC Nunn may have been acting on a 'gut feeling' about Gardiner and his potential involvement. Further proof that the police suspected Gardiner from the very beginning can be found within the pages of Superintendent George Andrews' work journal. Andrews, who was stationed at Halesworth, was the nearest senior officer to the murder and his journal entry for Sunday 1 June clearly shows that himself and Eli Nunn, on the day of the discovery of the body, were faced with a murder and that Gardiner was their number one suspect. He noted the following:

Sunday 1 June.
Office duty in the morning. At 1pm called by PC Nunn to Peasenhall in consequence of the body of a single woman having been found dead in the kitchen of her master house Mr Wm Crisp at Peasenhall.

Arrived at 2.30pm found the body was that of Roseanne Harsent aged 23 years. The throat was cut from left to right severing the windpipe and left jugular vein. The flannelette nightdress worn by the deceased was partially burned as was also the chemise. A quantity of broken glass was found near the body which was that of a 10oz Doctor Medicine Bottle. A letter was found in deceased's bedroom which was written by some person but not signed, asking for deceased to put her candle in the bedroom window at 10pm to leave it there for 10 minutes and that the writer would call on her at the back way around 12 o clock. A man named William Gardiner is suspected. Returned to station at 6pm. Reported to head Quarters and at 6.40pm en route to LONDON. [sic]

Of great note here is that Andrews only knew the basic details of the case, with the body only recently having been found, and so it wasn't known yet that Gardiner's family name was on the medicine bottle, or that the written letter found at the scene bore resemblance to two letters from Gardiner in Rose's drawer, or that Rose was, in fact, six months pregnant.

That being said, it was very strange that Gardiner would become the prime suspect in the case from what Andrews and Nunn had observed that afternoon alone and one can only speculate that perhaps Nunn had drawn this conclusion because he was a local resident and made an assumption based on the scandal between the two, but for Andrews to state this in his journal was a risk. He would have known that the journal was inspected on a regular basis by his Chief Constable but also, Andrews was no newbie to the job; he had joined the force in 1869 and was just one year away from retiring so, being a veteran of the force, he would surely not base his decision upon village gossip.

Mrs Gardiner was first interviewed on Monday, 2 June while her husband was at work. Eli Nunn was joined by Inspector Henry Berry of Halesworth and Sergeant Daniel Scarfe of Saxmundham, who made their way to see her between 10.00 and 11.00am and, at the same time, PC Scott was stationed at the Seed Drill Works to make sure Gardiner did not attempt to speak to his wife, an event which might impact her testimony. It appears that Nunn had made the decision to visit Gardiner's wife early because Superintendent George Sydney Staunton had wired him earlier that morning saying he hoped to arrive in Peasenhall around noon from Ipswich; it may be interesting to know that Staunton made the 24 mile trip to Peasenhall from Ipswich riding a bicycle. Staunton was given the case because crimes of murder were dealt with at Ipswich and he was the region's highest ranking officer to deal with the case.

It was also this afternoon that Rose's body was transported by van from Sibton to St Michael's church where the Reverend Ernest Cooke, the vicar, performed the funeral service. Following the ceremony the coffin was carried the short distance of a quarter of a mile through the narrow lanes to her final resting place within the cemetery.

Berry led with the questions, asking Mrs Gardiner, 'what time did your husband leave home on Saturday?' Georgianna replied that he had driven to Kelsale with Mr Rickards in the afternoon, then on to Leiston before returning home at around 9.30pm. Next he inquired about the type of writing paper the family used. Mrs Gardiner went away and then returned with an ordinary packet of penny writing-paper, but the time she was gone seemed highly suspicious to the policemen and they thought that she very well may have been hiding evidence by providing a basic writing paper and concealing the paper that they believed was used for the note.

Staunton arrived at Peasenhall shortly before 1.00pm and was immediately shown the letters found in Rose's drawer and after reading them he made his way to the drill works to interview Gardiner. Accounts later showed that Gardiner was very cooperative with the questions posed to him and replied in a calm way with no agitation in his replies. Staunton showed Gardiner the letters and asked him to show a sample of his writing, so Gardiner pulled out the notebook in which he recorded the time shifts of the workers and wages. Staunton noted the similarities in the writing, and whilst Gardiner did admit he could see a resemblance, he stated he had not written the note. At this point Staunton showed the second letter to Gardiner, which referred to the chapel incident, and Gardiner immediately said that was written in his own hand. At this point Staunton mentioned the similarity with the words 'you' and 'again' written in the letters and on the assignation note, but Gardiner made no comment on the matter. Staunton then asked Gardiner of his movements on the Saturday only to be given the same exact account given by Mrs Gardiner to the officers earlier that day. At this point Staunton decided to interview Mrs Gardiner himself and left the drill works, taking Nunn and Berry with him whilst Sergeant Scarfe was left to join Constable Scott in making sure Gardiner stayed at work.

Upon their return, Georgianna was somewhat unnerved to see the police for a second time that day and inquired as to where her husband was. She assumed he'd be home as usual before Staunton asked her once more about the movements of her husband on Saturday. She again gave the exact same story as earlier and also stated they had both gone to Mrs Dickinson's at 11.00pm and stayed with her until 1.30am as she was scared of the storm and needed comfort. Thus a perfect alibi was created for the evening. She was shown the envelope which had contained the assignation note and when asked if it was her husband's handwriting she said no but did state there was a similarity between the styles, and with this the officers left. They returned again at 4pm, at which point the focus of their questioning was the medicine bottle found at the murder scene. Georgianna asked what medicine bottle they were referring to. Staunton then put it to her that her sister had stayed with them earlier in the year and had been prescribed medicine from Dr Lay, Georgianna affirmed this to be correct. When asked why Rose should have had a bottle in her possession belonging to Georgianna's sister, she replied that she had given Rose some camphorated oil to treat a sore throat earlier in the year. Naturally, it seemed very peculiar that Rose should have in her possession a medicine bottle intended for Mrs Culham (Georgianna's sister). This was simply the police's assumption, rather than actual evidence, because of the blood-smeared label not being readable, but even worse was to come when it was revealed that after the label had been cleaned by police, the label read that the bottle contents were in fact intended for the Gardiners' children. This now became very damning evidence against them both because Mrs Gardiner had said it belonged to her sister, rather than her.

PC Nunn also made an important discovery that day when he learned that both Wright and Skinner lodged with Wright's stepfather, Harry Redgrift, a market gardener by trade whose brother, George, was a gamekeeper for Captain Levett-Scrivener. A man named James Morris worked for both brothers as an assistant gamekeeper during the season and gardener when required at other times. On the Sunday morning, Morris had told George Redgrift that at 5.00 am after the storm he had been walking up The Street from east to west before turning up Heveningham Road. It became more interesting when he passed by Gardiner's cottage where he noticed footprints in the muddy road. They began at the cottage, continuing down to Providence House and then appeared to return back to the cottage. Morris was intrigued and crossed over the road at Providence House and observed that the footprints went up to the gate of the house and also came away from there. He also noted that the imprint in the mud was made with a barred sole which could only mean it was made by a sole of rubber. Morris mentioned this to George Redgrift later that day.

Superintendent George Staunton paid another visit to Gardiner on 4 June, taking with him the second letter referring to the scandal. Strangely, he didn't suggest to Gardiner that this letter and note referring to the candle were both written in very similar styles. He instead compared the note with other examples of Gardiner's handwriting and compared only two words, 'you' and 'again'. But of course the letter was highly likely to have been disguised by the author in an attempt to conceal their identity.

The Inquest

The coroner's inquest began at the Swan Inn on Tuesday, 3 June. Such events in this period were held to determine whether a case should be followed through by a police investigation or that the cause of death had been by suicide or some other form of misadventure. The purpose of the inquest was to answer four questions: 1. Identification of the deceased; 2. The place of death; 3. The time of death; and 4. How the deceased came by their end.

The inquest was opened by the coroner, Mr C.W. Chaston. At the brief inquest Rose's parents gave evidence; William Harsent described the events surrounding the discovery of his daughter and identified the body. Rose's mother said that Rose had been engaged to be married since 1900 and that some weeks before her death they had asked her if she was pregnant, to which Rose replied that she was not. Mrs Crisp detailed the events of the night of 31 May. Others who spoke were Eli Nunn, who detailed what he saw upon arriving at Providence House, and both Dr Lay and Dr R..Richardson described the wounds inflicted upon Rose. Dr Lay was prevented from mentioning the label of the bottle at this time by Superintendent Staunton. Upon adjourning the inquest for a fortnight to give time for the police to continue their investigation, as well as time for the doctors to preform an in-depth post-mortem, the coroner noted that the assignation note posed a major problem when regarding the initial cause of death to be a suicide.

On this day it is interesting to know that Gardiner must have been beginning to feel the pressure of the circumstances because he went to work but instead of performing his usual duties, he was seen standing upon the gantry that overlooked the works, and at midday he said he felt ill and went home. As can be imagined, the gossipmongers took this as a sure sign of guilt and at 8.30pm that evening, Staunton, Nunn, Berry and Scarfe went to Gardiner's home to arrest him. The arresting officer was Nunn (as he had been the first officer at the scene on Sunday) who read the magistrate's warrant and cautioned him, to which Gardiner responded, 'I am innocent', before fainting on the sofa. He was revived with brandy and both Staunton and Nunn requested from Mrs Gardiner his clothes that were worn on the day of the murder. This was of course in the days of very primitive forensics, but a murder involving a slit throat would no doubt result in blood covering the clothes of the murderer. She provided them with a shirt, undershirt, vest and coat. They asked if any garment had been washed since Saturday to which she replied, no, she washed once a fortnight and her washing day was a week ahead. The kitchen knives were also removed to be examined. As Gardiner was led out of the house, she, too, fainted. Gardiner was taken six and half miles to Halesworth police station where he was searched. Within his trouser pocket was found a large clasp-knife. Gardiner was then remanded to Saxmundham petty sessions (petty sessions were minor courts that were presided over by two or more magistrates and were held in England from Tudor times), before being sent to Ipswich jail.

Nunn was sent back to Gardiner's home to retrieve all of his boots and shoes and obtained a pair of boots and the carpet slippers he had worn at Mrs Dickinson's during the night of the storm. Nunn returned on Friday 6 and Saturday 7 June also, the first time to collect an old pair of canvas shoes with rubber soles after Nunn had learned that footprints had been seen that led from the Gardiners' cottage to Providence House, and another set appeared to be leading in the opposite direction. The shoe imprint was said to be barred, which could only mean they were made of rubber. On Saturday, Nunn asked Georgianna for Gardiner's mackintosh, which Mrs Gardiner said would be found at the drill works. On Sunday the 8th Nunn requested a letter written by Gardiner to his wife which Georgianna was hesitant to pass on but did so upon condition the letter was returned within a week. It was at this point Georgianna consulted a solicitor, Mr Arthur Sadler Leighton, and his first job was to cease the daily visits Nunn was accustomed to, considering the police now had in their possession everything they could obtain. The Coroner's inquest resumed on 16 June, when a crucial point of evidence was discussed; the medicine bottle. After cleaning, it was found that the label on the medicine bottle in Rose's possession had been issued for the Gardiners' children. The foreman of the jury mentioned that this had not been spoken of at the first inquest and Mr Leighton jumped on the chance to get an answer from Dr Lay who was now of the opinion that death had been due to foul play.

Both Dr Lay and Dr Richardson had been of the opinion of suicide but were now conclusively of the belief that Rose had not attempted suicide. This was no doubt enhanced by Dr Richardsons' findings more than the word of Dr Lay whom one could argue was apparently incompetent.

Also of importance was a statement obtained from Mrs Crisp by Mr Leighton. Mrs Crisp said she heard Rose's scream during the middle of the storm, and she believed the time was between 1.00 and 2.00am; As both Mr and Mrs Gardiner were with Mrs Dickinson until at least 1.30am that night, this is very important. Also relayed at the inquest was that Andrews, on the previous Thursday evening, had placed a candle in Rose's window and Nunn had walked from Gardiner's doorstep until he could see the candle illuminating the window, moving a total of two yards until he could see it. This was done to act as a reconstruction of the events of the night of the murder and to test whether what Burgess had said could be plausible. After this Mr Leighton declared for the record that there was 'not a scrap of evidence against anybody'. The inquest was again adjourned until 30 June and was to be held at the new venue of Mr Smyth's Swiss Chalet assembly hall.

In the meantime, Gardiner appeared before the magistrates court at Saxmundham on 20 June. On the bench were J.K. Brooke of Sibton Park (chairman), Lieutenant Colonel H. Abdy Collins of Saxmundham and H.M. Doughty of Theberton. It was at this hearing that it would be decided whether the evidence held against Gardiner was strong enough to send him to trial at the Assizes or whether he was an innocent man with nothing more than circumstantial evidence against him. The prosecution was in the hands of an Ipswich Solicitor, E.P. Ridley, and in a statement made by him at the beginning of the trial he stated that for the past year Gardiner and Rose Harsent had been having 'immoral relations'. Mr Leighton, the defence, jumped up instantly and objected to Mr Ridley's claim unless he could bring forward witnesses to prove it. 'Of course I am going to call them', Mr Ridley responded. Mr Leighton continued to try and get the case dismissed and relentlessly objected to many statements made by Mr Ridley by saying that all the evidence against Gardiner was circumstantial. Mr Ridley stated that the murderer had brought with him a medicine bottle filled with paraffin in order to burn the body after he had committed the murder. The cork was, however, wedged tightly in the bottle neck and he could not open it and so he took the kitchen lamp to dismantle in order to extract paraffin from its well. He also noted the copy of the *East Anglian Daily Times* which was a newspaper read in the Gardiner house but not in the Crisp household. He noted the envelope that contained the note for Rose to leave her candle in the window: Gardiner would have had easy access to these envelopes as they were the same used at Smyth's Drill Works. Mr Ridley also mentioned the knife that was taken from Gardiner on the day of his arrest that was later found to have blood upon it even though an attempt had been made to clean it. Upon closer inspection however, it could not be determined if it was human blood (forensics were not that advanced at this time). Ridley also said that the postman and Mrs Crisp would confirm the delivery of letters like the assignment note being delivered to Rose at Providence House. He then implied that Rose's pregnancy had been the obvious motive for the murder and suggested that Gardiner had murdered Rose after he and his wife had returned from Mrs Dickinson's and as soon as his wife fell asleep, Gardiner slipped out of bed and made his way to Providence House. The statement he provided about the distinctive footprints leading from Gardiner's house to Providence House and back also provided very strong – but still circumstantial – evidence.

PC Nunn also spoke and, in addition to previous statements, added that upon searching Rose's bedroom in more detail he had found a stack of letters within her drawer; the two letters from Gardiner and several indecent letters and poems that were written by Frederick Davis, a 19-year-old grocer boy at Emmett's store who made deliveries to Providence House twice a week and also saw Rose at the chapel at Sibton each week. It is very important to note at this stage that the number of letters found in Rose's room totalled twenty-six. Of these, we know of Gardiner's letters, as well as a total of six written by Davis, and it is safe to assume Rose would have retained letters from family members also but we can safely determine that Rose was also receiving correspondence from at least one other man. This fact was to be an aid later to the prosecution at trial to display Rose in an unfavourable light – a woman not as demure as many others believed.

Mrs Crisp – who had previously been able to give a time of the scream she'd heard – had seemingly retracted her statement given at the inquest and this was to fuel the attack on her by Mr Leighton who wasted no time in a relentless and prolonged cross-examination. Her new evidence was that she could not be so sure of the time she'd heard the scream. She also now stated that because of the torrential rain and thunder, she could not hear the clock chime at midnight after all. This played straight into the hands of the prosecution because as Dr Lay could not determine an accurate time of death on the morning of 1 June when he examined the body, the prosecution could now place the time of death in a wider time frame. Mr Leighton put it to Mrs Crisp that she had been encouraged to change her statement by both Staunton and Ridley. She denied this but was unable to give a satisfactory answer as to why she was so sure of the time before but now could not be so certain.

The postman, Frederick Brewer, was to testify that Rose had asked him if she had a letter in his delivery on Saturday, 31 May and he stated that she had never approached him before to ask him about mail deliveries. When asked if he'd ever delivered letters in envelopes similar to the one she received on that Saturday he could not be certain.

Harry Harsent, Rose's younger brother, was to testify that he had taken letters from Gardiner to Rose the previous year and that they were always in blue envelopes; he had carried replies from Rose to Gardiner also, though again, of the number he could not be certain. Of note in his statement is that he regularly obtained the *East Anglian Daily Times* from Emmett's shop and took it to Gardiner at his workplace.

Bricklayer Harry Burgess told how he'd met Gardiner in the street and that he had observed the candlelight in Rose's window at 10pm.

Mrs Dickinson confirmed that the Gardiners had come to sit with her during the storm at 11.30pm and had left her at 1.30am. The gamekeeper, James Morris, went on to describe the distinctive footprints he'd seen that led from the Gardiners' cottage to Providence House and back again in the rain-sodden mud.

The best witness was to be saved for last – Bill Wright. He retold the evening in May 1901 when he and Skinner had overheard the liaison between Rose and Gardiner at the Doctor's Chapel. He simply said, 'laughing and talking in the Chapel.' To Mr Leighton, Bill Wright was one of the two men who could destroy his defence quite easily and quickly, and so, in a bullying fashion, he began his cross-examination: 'Have you played the part of an eavesdropper before? An amateur detective, in fact?' Wright gave no reply. Mr Leighton continued, 'Do you often make it your business to pry into other people's doings?' The magistrates court (where the inquest was being held) was adjourned after this for another two weeks.

On 30 June at the assembly hall a third attempt was made to conclude the issue. This time, several statements had been changed yet again, all to be seemingly more damning against the accused. Mrs Dickinson, who previously claimed that Mrs Gardiner had arrived with her at 11.30pm, now said Gardiner didn't arrive until around midnight. She now also stated she had seen Rose carrying a parcel to Gardiner's cottage at around 9pm on that Saturday, but as far as she knew, both the Gardiners were not at home. Harry Harsent's evidence also changed; upon reflection, he said he had actually taken letters from Rose to Gardiner in 1901 from June onwards. He still didn't know the total he carried but he recalled taking a further two in 1902. All were in blue envelopes. He had taken replies to Gardiner from Rose too, but not within the last twelve months.

The factory manager, John Samuel Rickards, gave his evidence and said that Gardiner had easy access to the office envelopes like the one that had contained the assignment note. This claim was quickly swept away however when Captain Levett-Scrivener pointed out that he used similar envelopes himself and that the envelopes were not that unusual.

Mr Leighton was to ascertain from Superintendent Staunton that Gardiner's clothes were taken from his house and, in addition to this, the police had also conducted a search of a well behind Gardiner's home. He revealed that all the letters found with Rose's possessions were in the hands of the leading handwriting expert in the country, Mr Thomas Gurrin. It was at this point it was revealed that Fred Davis had penned the obscene poems and letters. Unsurprisingly, this caused a stir amongst the jurors as it seemed that there was a potential new suspect in the case, maybe he was a jilted lover? Mr Cooke, the vicar, who was one of the jurors, asked if Davis had provided a satisfactory account of his movements on the night of 31 May. Staunton replied that he had done so and that Davis had been at home. This understandably would have created a few raised eyebrows.

Now came the two men, Wright and Skinner. It appears that Wright had added to his previous statement by saying he had heard Rose at the Doctor's Chapel cry, 'oh, oh!' which was then followed by some rustling about. This was obviously very important information that had not been mentioned before at the original inquest. Mr Leighton again wasted no time in mentioning this to Wright when he cross-examined him. Wright's only defence was to say he had only answered the questions put to him at the time and they had not asked him any questions relating to the noise at the chapel, nor any words spoken by Rose. Also to appear again were Lay and Nunn who spoke only to state that Gardiner's knife found on his person at his arrest, could have inflicted the wounds on Rose but that the table knife they had taken away from the murder scene on the day of Gardiner's arrest could not possibly have caused the fatal wounds. After this it was strongly suggested by the coroner that the inquest should close and that the jury not return with an open verdict or, by definition, a jury affirming the occurrence of a suspicious death but not specifying the cause, because the jury could easily dismiss the case and believe Gardiner's excuse for him using it to skin a rabbit.

Just 30 minutes later they returned with a guilty verdict. It was not quite over yet though because the defence fully intended to exercise their right to overturn the verdict at trial. The last chance to clear Gardiner's name would be at an appeal to be held on 3 July at Saxmundham Magistrates.

It was at this appeal that Alfonso Skinner faced the frustrations of Mr Leighton. Mr Leighton knew his back was now against the wall and his line of questioning was blunt and full of heavy tones of sarcasm as these three questions show most clearly:

'Why didn't you tell the coroner's jury about this interview with Gardiner?'

'The usual thing – because I was not asked!'

'Have you had your memory refreshed lately? Why didn't you say before the coroner that you caught Gardiner up and walked with him?'

Mr Gurrin gave his opinion on the handwriting upon the envelopes. He would only conclude that they were similar but would not conclusively claim that the note delivered to Rose on that Saturday had been written by Gardiner's hand.

Finally, Dr John Stevenson of the Home Office revealed his findings of the evidence provided to him, the broken medicine bottle which had contained paraffin and the knife that had been retrieved from Gardiner on the Sunday morning following the murder on the previous night. He confirmed that the medicine bottle was not used to inflict any injury on Rose and that the clasp-knife did have blood on it but it could not be determined if this was animal blood or human blood, let alone Rose's. He noted that no blood nor paraffin was found on any of Gardiner's clothing by the police.

The Magistrates decided that the original verdict was to be held and he was sent for trial at the Assizes. Gardiner was mentally exhausted from the inquests and he knew now that a conviction at his future trial would result in his being hung for the murder of Rose Hersent. He was allowed a little time with his wife Georgianna and was seen crying with her before he was taken back to Ipswich prison via train.

Chapter Five

The First Trial

William Gardiner's trial began at Suffolk Assizes in Ipswich Shire Hall on Thursday, 6 November 1902. The prosecution was to be led by Mr H.F. Dickens KC, who was the son of the great novelist Charles Dickens, and the Hon John De Grey. The defence counsel was led by E.E. Wild and Mr E.H. Claughton Scott. The judge who presided over the proceedings was Sir William Grantham, a former conservative member of Parliament.

At 10.30am Judge Grantham began the trial. William Gardiner – wearing a dark suit and sporting a neatly trimmed beard – took his place in the dock, sitting in an armchair. Court reporters noted that he showed great interest in each of the jurors as they were sworn in. The prosecution opened proceedings, and Mr Dickens began by giving a brief account of the case before Gardiner. He said that there had been 'an immoral intercourse' between Gardiner and Rose which had carried on long after the incident at Sibton Chapel and had eventually led to her later becoming pregnant. He said that by May 1902, her pregnancy was becoming increasingly difficult to conceal and, with this set of circumstances now facing Gardiner that the man in the dock had written a final letter asking to meet Rose at Providence House at midnight on that Saturday night, before murdering her and trying to burn her body.

After this Mr Dickens went much further into the case and named all of the individuals who he would be calling and gave a brief summary of their anticipated testimonies. Mr Dickens was stopped once by the defence when Mr Wild heard that the prosecution was intending to read a letter from Henry Rouse – another pillar of the Methodist church – that had been sent to Gardiner after Rouse had allegedly seen Rose and Gardiner playing footsie at the chapel. Mr Wild's protestation was that the letter was both undated and unsigned and therefore couldn't be proven to be from Rouse, to which Mr Dickens noted it was in fact dated 14 April 1902. Wild hit back quickly, stating that this evidence had not been heard until 1 November. Mr Dickens returned with 'I think I had better not read the letter', to which Mr Wild strongly said, 'I don't mind my friend reading it at all'. The letter was not produced at trial.

Continuing in his address, Dickens then referred to the fact Mrs Crisp had received a tough time from Mr Leighton previously and told the jury the importance of understanding exactly what Mrs Crisp had stated on two occasions previously.

Substantially, before the coroner she said she thought it was between 1am and 2am when she heard a scream (supposedly from Rose) and thud. Before the Magistrates however, Mrs Crisp said she was asleep and therefore had no means of judging what the actual time was. It was an undoubted fact from the evidence he should later call that the prisoner and his wife from 12am until 1.30am were in Mrs Dickinson's house, as corroborated by Mrs Dickinson herself.

Mr Dickens, by making this statement was, of course, trying to clear any confusion about the timings of the scream and thud heard during the night of the great tempest because he knew that Mrs Crisp not being able to confirm the time could easily get Gardiner off the hook, since his whereabouts had not been accounted for from 1.30am to 2am. Mr Dickens stated that because of one of the worst storms in memory occurring that night it is very plausible that Gardiner would have been delayed in meeting Rose at the arranged time because of the unpredictable events which meant he could well have gone to Providence House later than the letter had called for. It was also of note that both PC Nunn and Dr Lay stated that Rose's bed had not been slept in. She had obviously greatly anticipated this meeting and wanted to see the person who had sent the letter and would later murder her – it was a meeting of such importance that she didn't turn in for the night to await the meeting to be arranged at a later date.

Mr Dickens then called his first witness, Superintendent Andrews, and displayed maps of Peasenhall and plans of the layout of Providence House and the Doctor's Chapel that Andrews went into great detail over. This was to illustrate how the murderer would have behaved, the routes taken by him and so on. Next was Bill Wright, one of the two men who had begun the original rumour amongst the village, who went over his events of that evening at the Doctor's Chapel. After a little bit of digging, the defence discovered that Wright had made similar accusations before and so Mr Wild was quick as a fox in the following attack:

Wild	Have you never gone about what is called 'garping' in the country – seeing what's going on between young men and women?
Wright	I think not.
Wild	Don't you know?
Wright	I know I have not.
Wild	Let me just remind you. Don't you remember the time a few years ago when a young man named Ernest Cady was going to be married to a young woman?

Note: Ernest Cady was Georgianna's brother – a possible indication that Wright had some sort of vendetta against the family.

Wright	I know him well.
Wild	Did you say then you saw them go into an orchard and behave improperly?
Wright	No, Sir.
Wild	What were you doing? Weren't you up in a tree?

Wright	I was gathering apples. (Laughter in the courtroom)
Wild	Did you spread a scandal about these two people then?
Wright	No, we mentioned it, but we did not mention any scandal about it.
Wild	Did Cady come and ask you what it meant?
Wright	Cady never came to me.
Wild	Did Cady's mother ask you what you meant?
Wright	Yes, Cady's mother did.
Wild	Did you say there was another young fellow with you and he saw the same thing?
Wright	I can't recollect. It was years ago.
Wild	Was it true that you saw this indecency then?
Wright	I never said anything about indecency.
Wild	You thought that was bad?
Wright	No.
Wild	What did you talk about it for?
Wright	(No response).

This back-and-forth was a double-edged sword because whilst it inferred that Wright was a gossip monger with a possible dislike for the Gardiner family, it also revealed that he had not actually reported seeing any indecency going on at the orchard, so he wasn't prone to exaggerating the events he happened to fall upon. Nevertheless, Wright was left embarrassed and the prosecution team must have sat uncomfortably during the exchange.

Alphonso Skinner, the other man who had been a witness to the Doctor's Chapel incident, was not scorned as Wright was by the defence since he had nothing in his past that made his testimony questionable. He retold his story as he had done before but made one addition this time by stating he had heard Gardiner say 'Don't say anything about it. I shall be here tomorrow at 8 o'clock'. This was to be the conclusion of day one.

Day two began with Mr John Guy describing the enquiry at the chapel and the visit Gardiner had made to him later on when Gardiner had decided that the legal route against both Wright and Skinner was futile. The defence made no attack on Mr Guy and the prosecution didn't pick up on anything of note either, despite the fact that it certainly appeared that Gardiner may very well have tried to double bluff Wright and Skinner into recanting their statements.

After this missed opportunity by both counsels, the next person to take the stand was Preacher Henry Rouse. He recalled stories of Rose and Gardiner acting in a way much akin to being a couple rather than just friends speaking particularly of Gardiner putting his feet in Rose's lap at chapel on one occasion. The aforementioned letter Rouse had written to Gardiner, although dated, was a problem since he had not signed it, nor in fact had he written it; it transpired that Rouse had dictated the wording to his wife who then wrote the letter on his behalf. The reason for this is unclear, but it was likely that he wanted to alert Gardiner to what was becoming widely known, yet didn't want to be associated with the scandal in any way. This instantly angered Judge Grantham because Rouse had not penned or signed this evidence. After all, how would Gardiner possibly know who had written the letter? Gardiner wouldn't recognize the writing so it would have just appeared to him to have been an anonymous letter from a busybody. Mr Rouse was left embarrassed also.

Now it came to the letters that Rose had in her possession upon her death. Frederick Brewer, the local postman, was questioned. He stated that on the morning of Saturday, 31 May, Rose had approached him and enquired if there was any delivery for her; this was an important statement because Rose was not in the habit of asking Brewer if he had letters for her. At around 3.15pm he delivered a letter to Rose – the assignation note that was within a buff envelope – and he told the court he had delivered five, if not six, similar letters within the past twelve months and up to three of those had been in 1902. It is here that a very interesting piece of information should be noted. The envelope was postmarked with a

Yoxford stamp and this indicates that the letter was either written and then posted at Yoxford for delivery to Peasenhall, or that the letter was written and posted in Peasenhall but then for some reason was missed as a local delivery before being sent the four miles to Yoxford and then returned to Peasenhall to be delivered. Rose had no correspondents in Yoxford, so the letter must be assumed to be fact, and that would mean the letter would have been posted in Peasenhall between 6.30 pm on Friday 30 May and 10.30am, Saturday 31 May. Another point to raise is that Peasenhall is a small village and all locations there are easily accessible within a few minutes of walking so the people of Peasenhall wishing to write to their fellow villagers would usually hand deliver such items. This clearly meant that the author of this particular letter did not want to be seen delivering the note in person; the actions of a calculating individual.

Rose's younger brother, Harry Harsent, was called to confirm his previous statements that he had taken 'two or three' letters from Gardiner to Rose in 1901 that were within blue envelopes and that he had also taken letters from his sister to Gardiner in 1902 but none had been replied to by Gardiner. The skeleton of the case was now established. Now it was time to add the frame and tie Gardiner to the tragic events that had occurred on that late spring evening.

Mrs Crisp was called to the stand to describe the events at Providence House that evening. Mrs Crisp was a nervous woman by nature and a trait of this nervousness was, unfortunately, to laugh when asked serious questions; it had happened at the inquest and now this affliction raised its head once more under oath in the courtroom. Mrs Crisp said she had gone to bed at 10.15pm and had said 'goodnight' to Rose, who was in the hall at the time. Mrs Crisp noticed that Rose was holding a candlestick that she used for her bedroom and a lamp for use in the kitchen. Of note here is the lamp that was kept on the kitchen table. Mr Wild asked if she took the *East Anglian Daily Times* (this was the paper that had been rolled up and placed under the head of Rose and set alight in the attempt to burn the body) to which Mrs Crisp said no. Mr Wild asked Mrs Crisp if she remembered saying to her husband about the scream and thud, 'I wonder if it is Rose? Shall I go to her?' and that her husband replied, 'No if she's nervous she'll come to us.' By now the nerves were seemingly getting to Mrs Crisp, as she responded that she had no recollection of the statement. Mr Wild angrily rebuked her by saying, 'This is a matter of vital importance to me and my client – couldn't you have been paying attention when you were sworn before the Coroner?' Mrs Crisp offered no response.

Herbert Stammers, a neighbour of the prisoner, was called and retold himself seeing Gardiner on the Sunday morning at 7.30am as he walked towards his washhouse. Stammers noted Gardiner lighting a fire there. When asked if he'd seen this occur on a regular basis he confirmed that he had, and later confirmed that the washhouse was surrounded by properties belonging to Mrs Pepper, Mrs Gardiner, Mrs Dickinson and others. Mr Stammers then left the dock whereupon an argument broke out amongst the counsels that Mr Stammers had, on the morning of the 1st, seen a great fire in the washhouse. The judge then decided to recall Mr Stammers to the dock. Upon returning to the witness box, the judge questioned him about the great fire he'd seen:

Stammers	Well, I thought it an excellent blaze.
Judge	You mean a large blaze?
Stammers	Yes.
Judge	Why did you think so?
Stammers	Because I thought it was larger than I had seen in an ordinary way.
Mr Wild	Why did you not tell the jury that in your evidence just now?
Stammers	They never asked me that.

Mr Wild then asked to recall Mrs Dickinson, and when the judge enquired why, Mr Wild declared that she may have noticed something curious about the fire since she lived nearby.

Mrs Dickinson was sitting amongst the spectators and was ordered to stand before being questioned, but she explained that she slept in her front bedroom, and would not have seen the fire at that time. She told the judge she awoke at 8am on that Sunday morning. Mr Wild then asked if she'd gone to the wash house at the back, to which Mrs Dickinson replied, 'I don't often do so on Sunday mornings'.

William Harsent then spoke to describe the scene that he found on the Sunday morning but provided no further items of interest that he hadn't stated at the inquest previously.

To conclude the second day's proceedings, Mr Thomas Gurrin, the handwriting expert, was called. He gave evidence of his comparisons of the anonymous letter, the midnight rendezvous and the letters that Gardiner had admitted to writing; with seventeen years experience, Gurrin was confident that the letters had all been penned by the same person. Mr Wild, knowing that Mr Gurrin's evidence could sway the jury, quickly pointed out the spacing of the words in the assignation letter compared to the two other letters written by Gardiner was different and that the assignation note had been written by someone else. Mr Gurrin held his opinion but faltered when Mr Wild said that both of Gardiner's letters were written in a superior style to the assignation letter by agreeing with him. With this the court was adjourned until 10am the following morning.

Day three was the day the defence had to pull out all the stops as the evidence against Gardiner was piling up. Mr Wild spoke to the jurors to reiterate the seriousness of the case and the fact that their decision would potentially either exonerate Gardiner or leave Mrs Gardiner a widow and their children without a father. He went on to criticise Wright as he had left the scene of the Doctor's Chapel on more than one occasion on that night. He attacked Skinner too, wondering why he had amended his statement by saying he'd heard Gardiner speak days after the original statement. Mr Wild said of the slanderous actions that neither Wright nor Skinner could recant their claims as it would prove them to be liars and, after all, the two of them together clearly outnumbered Gardiner. He attacked

Mr Rouse who, while preaching in the rostrum in the chapel, said he saw Gardiner and Rose sitting side by side before Gardiner placed his legs on Rose's knees. Rouse continued his sermon, saying nothing before then sending Gardiner an anonymous letter that was unsigned and written by his wife after he dictated it to her. He then moved on to the community of Peasenhall and how such a small village could revel in scandals such as this. He also said that 'Mrs Gardiner has disbelieved the story all through, and has stuck to her husband, and been friendly to the girl up to the time that the murder was committed'.

His focus then moved on to the night of the murder. He mentioned the very important evidence submitted by Mrs Dickinson who had testified to both the Gardiners sitting with her through the storm. They had stayed until 1.30am, with Gardiner appearing to be calm and collected at the time he left. His calm demeanour was most important – if Gardiner was the murderer, wouldn't he have been on edge? Wouldn't he realise that the time window in which he had to commit the murder was running out because of the impending dawn? As the judge had previously asked Mrs Dickinson, 'How do you know it was half-past one?' Mrs Dickinson replied, 'There is an hour and a half to daylight', this of course is true because at three o'clock in the morning at that time of year it is indeed light. There is in fact just a seven minute difference between sunrise on June 1st to Midsummer's Day on the 21st. Given the fact of the time of death was reported at 8 am and Gardiner and his wife were reported to have gone home to bed after the storm at 2 am, then Gardiner getting up and creeping out of his own house, going to Providence House, committing the murder and returning home would mean that Gardiner did all this within an hour as he would not have wanted to be out and seen as twilight began.

Mr Wild was quick in delivering his own verdict of exactly who the father of Rose's child was: Frederick Davis. Davis was the 'boy next door' to Rose and had been the author of some rather risque letters that, he claimed, were written at Rose's request. Mr Wild said, 'I do suggest to you that, if it is a question of who was the father of the child, one can have very little doubt he was in the witness box yesterday'. This would surely cast doubt on the motive of the murder if the baby wasn't William Gardiner's.

Mrs Gardiner was then called to the witness box. It appeared that she was delivering answers from a well-rehearsed script, after all, she had been forced to repeat the account of the fateful night so many times over the four months from the murder to the trial to perfect her alibi for her husband. Mrs Gardiner confirmed the events on the night of the storm; her husband had gone to the doorstep at 10pm to watch the storm as it gathered pace, he was wearing carpet slippers and did indeed also follow her to Mrs Dickinson's house to sit with the terrified woman. She stated they later returned home and as they were undressing for bed, the clock struck 2am, and that at 2.20am it was already starting to get light. Then after this their 6-year-old son Bertie awoke and cried for five or ten minutes, and when she returned to the bedroom after comforting him, her husband was asleep in bed. She went on to say that the pair woke at between 8 and 8.30am. When asked about the fire being lit in the wash house, she claimed it was to heat the kettle and that nothing else was burned, and that his movements for the rest of the day were completely normal.

It was now time for William Gardiner to take the stand at last. Gardiner spoke to confirm his age, occupation and his offices held within the Primitive Methodist Connexion. He also confirmed he'd known Rose for seven or eight years and that Rose was both a regular visitor to his house and a friend to his wife. Onlookers were impressed with his demeanour and confidence. Unsurprisingly, he spoke of his account of the fateful night exactly how his wife had done so short a while before him. When the subject of Wright and Skinner's testimony was raised, Gardiner was at a loss as to why they should have spoken of him in that way and could only offer a futile response that his employer, Mr Smyth, had previously reprimanded Wright for unsatisfactory work.

Gardiner stood firm in his questioning. All questions put to him were answered swiftly and with a confident tone and only one time did he deviate when he paused as Mr Wild asked about the incident when he supposedly placed his feet in Rose's lap, to which he retorted; 'Do I really want to answer that question?'.

Abraham Goddard came next to the witness box, a Methodist farmer who was to testify that the Doctor's Chapel inquest had been concluded as being nothing more than just idle gossip, but that he had been told by Mr Guy that the allegations made by Wright and Skinner were not mere fabrication, Guy was no doubt beginning to believe that there was no smoke without fire, no matter how much he wanted to believe Gardiner. After this the court was adjourned until Monday morning and the jurors were offered an outing on the Sunday to Felixstowe.

The trial began again on Monday morning with a request from the jurors – they wanted to see all letters written by Gardiner, from the ones he had sent to Rose to and including any written from prison. They specifically wanted letters written near the time of the murder, especially one Gardiner had written to his wife which had subsequently been returned to Mrs Gardiner at Peasenhall. Mr Wild offered to send a car to Peasenhall to obtain the letter with strict instructions to the driver to be as fast as he could and an assurance given to him that he would not face prosecution for breaking any speed limit. The driver returned by lunch after averaging a staggering 20mph at top speed.

Mr Wild then set about summing up the defence and, as before, had a scathing few words for Skinner, saying, 'of his own account.... A filthy young man who goes about searching for what vice and sin he can discover'. He said of the knife found on Gardiner that the idea it was the murder weapon 'was a pretty one – the sort of thing one reads in a comic paper' and if Dr Stevenson was to be believed about the age of blood stains that would have condemned many to the gallows. One hindering fact for the prosecution was the fact that no clothes with blood on them were ever discovered at Gardiner's house after his arrest when PC Nunn had called to collect evidence. The prosecution decided the reason for this was the fire on Sunday morning – did Gardiner burn any clothes that were worn during the murder? After all, given the nature of the crime, there would have been a great deal of blood on the murderer. The defence knew this lack of evidence was to their advantage.

Mr Wild reminded the jury that their duty was to only find his client guilty if they felt it was beyond reasonable doubt that he had committed the murder and concluded by saying:

> I need hardly point out that the verdict you give is not a collective but an individual verdict. It is not like a misdemeanour, for each of you is sworn separately to make a deliverance between our Sovereign Lord the King and the prisoner. I appeal to any man, if he believes that the prisoner is innocent, to let no consideration blind his eyes to the fact that he has individual responsibility.

Mr Dickens for the prosecution, a far more accomplished legal man, made his own statement as to why Rose had been murdered and then proceeded to do everything possible to incriminate Gardiner by saying:

> What conditions must be fulfilled in order to make the unknown man fit in with the circumstances of the case? He must have been the man who wrote the letter 'A' [assignation letter], who, according to the defence, wrote in a handwriting extraordinarily like the prisoner at the bar; who, on that night, wore indiarubber shoes and walked to and fro between the prisoner's house and Providence House, a man who had a knife similar to the kind of knife found in possession of the prisoner; who was curiously brought into connection with a medicine bottle bearing the words, 'Mrs Gardiner's children'; who got hold of those buff envelopes in order to write that letter making the assignation; who had the same reason to get rid of the woman as we have been able to prove the prisoner had; who must have been on the lookout for the light in the

window at ten o'clock, in the way that the prisoner was; he must have been a man of such position that it was imperative for him to conceal his shame as we say the prisoner's position was. It is my painful duty to point out these facts. Are all these coincidences? Is it probable that this unknown man who committed the murder fulfils all the conditions which in every case point to the prisoner at the bar?

Look at the other side of the case. The prisoner lives at Peasenhall, the prisoner writes remarkably like the letter 'A', he has indian rubber shoes corresponding to the marks of the footprints going to and fro on that terrible night, he has a knife which fulfils the condition which you would expect the knife to show by which that crime was committed, he has brought into natural communication with the medicine bottle because it is brought from his own house. The prisoner has access to the buff envelopes. The prisoner has reason to get rid of Rose Harsent if you believe the witness. The prisoner looked out for the light just at ten o'clock because, from his own evidence and the evidence of his family, he was in a position in which exposure would be fatal.

Mr Dickens summed up the prosecution beautifully. His argument was strong and he made claims that were almost impossible to ignore and when the all important question was made of the blood on the clothes, as obviously such a vicious attack would leave the attacker drenched in blood, Dickens mentioned that due to the fact there were no bloody footprints at the scene or near the house outside, the murderer must have taken off his shoes. He also performed a mime for the jury, showing how the murderer could have inflicted fatal wounds upon Rose to avoid being covered in her blood. He illustrated that an attack from the front would have resulted in the murderer being sprayed with blood being released at great pressure from the carotid artery and jugular vein, whereas if the murderer had knelt down beside the victim and to her side, he would have escaped the torrent of blood escaping the body and thus leaving the scene with no blood upon his clothing. Either one was quite bizarre given the blood had been measured to have spurted up to 2 feet beyond Rose's own feet where she fell.

The pleas from both counsels had been heard and now it was the turn of Judge Sir William Grantham to speak. The comments of a judge are supposed to be fair and not intended to sway the jury either way, but it seems his honour was rather damning towards Gardiner and it was clearly visible to those in attendance that Gardiner had a look of pure dejection on his face. The judge even went through the defence's case and quite clearly displayed his doubt in their points. He attacked Mr Crisp for not following up on his wife's instincts because had he done so, they could very well have prevented the murder. He then dismissed the Sibton Chapel inquiry as being prejudiced (this, of course, is very true). To the jury he expressed that if they believed the testimonies of both Wright and Skinner then they must address this as 'a very strong piece of additional evidence'. Regarding the issue of Davis being the father of Rose's unborn child, he said that there was 'not a tittle of evidence' to support this, again this was true, but there was also no real evidence that the child was Gardiner's, only speculation based on previous rumours.

When turning to Mrs Crisp, the judge said that the scream and thud were at the time of the murder and the fact that three witnesses – Mrs Dickinson, Mrs Gardiner and Mrs Pepper – had all said Gardiner was not near Providence House at that time was totally irrelevant. Quite how a judge could be allowed to portray his quite obvious contempt for the witnesses is baffling today, but these were times when a judge really was in control of his courtroom and a rather strict and no-nonsense approach could be taken by this senior of the judiciary system. He even did his own deducing, by saying as rigor mortis had set in when the body was inspected by Dr Lay, who therefore claimed death had occurred some four hours earlier, it was therefore entirely possible that Mrs Gardiner had fallen asleep by that point and not noticed her husband's absence and that Gardiner's footprints would have been easily found by Morris on the Sunday morning as the muddy paths were still wet from the deluge of the previous night's storm.

He also said that the evidence pointed to a relationship between Rose and Gardiner which gave him a need to dispose of Rose and their unborn child. He said that the copy of the *East Anglian Daily Times* should be disregarded, which was unusual given that the Crisp family hadn't taken the paper yet Gardiner did.

The medicine bottle was filled with paraffin and had a label that connected it to the Gardiner household. The judge didn't believe Rose had brought it to the kitchen but that the murderer had brought it with the full intention to use the contents to burn the body. He then openly disregarded Mrs Gardiner's claim that there was not a 'great fire', as Stammer had said, at 7.30am because they didn't awake until 8am. The jury was subconsciously torn between believing Mr Stammers or Mrs Gardiner, but the judge obviously believed the former witness.

It was now said and done by all parties. The jurors left the courtroom at 4.15pm with clearly mixed emotions but they had been very heavily influenced to pass a verdict of guilty upon the accused by the judge. William Gardiner had probably begun the day in high spirits as the defence, up to that point, seemed to clearly hold the upper hand, but by the concluding statements he must have quite literally been in fear for his life given the verbal attack by the so-called impartial judge. At 6.30pm the jury returned – just over two hours had elapsed which is never a good sign for a defendant. However, they returned to ask a question: what amount of thought should be given to the absence of blood on Gardiner's clothes and the fact there was no evidence he had destroyed any clothing whatsoever? Justice Grantham could only say that these circumstances would favour the prisoner but added that they were not to be viewed as conclusive. With this the jury returned to consider their verdict and at 8.40pm they returned again, with the foreman informing the court that they could not agree. Justice Grantham asked if he could aid them by answering any other questions whereupon one juror stood and said he had no questions to ask. The judge asked whether, if more time was given, they may reach full agreement. The juror replied that he had heard no evidence to find Gardiner guilty but nor had he heard any evidence to find him not guilty.

That was it, for a guilty verdict and the death penalty, all jurors would need to be in agreement and it was clear that nothing would sway the obstinate juror. The jury was dismissed and Gardiner was to be tried once again at the next Assizes. He was in a state of clear shock and almost fainted as he was led away. Who was this juror who had saved Gardiner from the death penalty? That was to be revealed by Superintendent Andrews who had recorded the trial in his work journal. For some reason though he had dated the case during the month of October instead of November and his entry for 10 November read as follows.

Monday 10 Oct.

IPSWICH ASSIZE. At 8.45pm the jury being unable to agree upon their verdict were discharged the being 11 against prisoner. The juror for him was Mr Evan Edwards of Felixstowe, who was and is against Capital Punishment. Mr Edwards was against 'Capital Punishment' it seems that Gardiner was destined to escape the gallows from day one of the trial and digging deeper it was also discovered that Mr Edwards was also a[n evangelical Christian.

It is also interesting to note that Mr Edwards was a close friend of Salvation Army founder General Booth and had walked beside him when he toured the streets of Ipswich receiving a far from friendly response, and after that the general even stayed with Edwards when he visited East Anglia. Mr Edwards had stood strong as his fellow jurors voted for a death sentence; he was not to be swayed in any way and stood by his own conviction. It was now down to another set of jurors to decide the fate of William Gardiner.

Chapter Six

The Second Trial

The second trial of William Gardiner was set to begin on Tuesday, 20 January 1903.

It had been just over two months since the previous trial that had voted eleven to one in favour of conviction and it seemed that this would have a detrimental effect on the second trial, but oddly the opposite appears to have been true. For example, the *Eastern Morning Gazette*'s editor wrote of Rose Harsent:

> Rose Harsent herself had not worn the white flower of a blameless Life. She appears to have revelled in the filthy verses whose author received a well-deserved castigation from the bench.

It was clear that public opinion had swayed away from the servant girl who had been so cruelly slain to a girl with a promiscuous side that invited the terrible events that befell her.

The East Anglian Times even opened a defence fund to support Georgianna Gardiner. With her husband sitting behind bars there was no income to support the family (she had even taken the bold step to write to *The Times* of London requesting aid as she was 'penniless and heartbroken'). In an ironic twist, Mr Evan Edwards, the man who had saved her husband ten weeks earlier, contributed the large sum of £20 to get the fund started. That is equivalent to £2,620 in today's money.

The paper kept the fund open until the conclusion of the trial; the total raised was just over £360 (roughly £47,147 today). The money ensured that Georgianna could be comfortable and allowed her to stay in Ipswich with her sister so that she could visit her husband who was imprisoned there.

The fear and anxiety that must have been going through Gardiner's mind would have been unbearable. He knew he'd escaped by the skin of his teeth the first time and now he must face it all again with the risk that this time, there may not be a juror opposed to the death penalty. The once strong man began to look depleted and frail.

In the two months between trials, Mr Wild made a personal visit to Peasenhall to visit the crime scene at Providence House where Mrs Crisp let him walk around. His assistant, Mr Leighton, accompanied him and his role was to hunt for gossip about Rose and for witnesses who favoured the prosecution. The prosecution, who knew they had been so close before, also went to Peasenhall in an attempt to find more witnesses that would deliver their victory.

On 24 November, Superintendent Andrews and PC Eli Nunn visited Sibton to speak with Henry Rouse. The statement he gave recalling Gardiner putting his feet in Rose's lap was deemed a vital one to the prosecution as it backed up Wright and Skinner's story, and so any other witness to this event would be a highly valuable asset.

Rouse pointed them in the direction of a Mr Thomas Hunt who lived beside the chapel. Mr Hunt, however, was not keen to relinquish any information he had and was of no use to the police. The note made by Andrews in his work journal says it all: 'conferred with Mr Hunt whose word I found was not to be trusted RE Gardiner. He being anxious to screen the Murderer at the expense of Justice'. This was always going to be a difficult task. The community of Sibton would be expected to close ranks. Gardiner, in their eyes, was a hard-working, married and respected man of the community. As far as they were concerned the inquest in 1902 had exonerated him entirely from any wrongdoing or scandals. After all, he was a man of God.

All images were supplied by Stewart Evans (Jack The Ripper expert and author) from his personal archive.

Alphonso Skinner, one of the two men who overheard the conversation between Rose and William at the Doctors Chapel.

The kitchen at Providence House, where the father of Rose Harsent found the body of his murdered daughter. The staircase, at the foot of which the body lay, leads to the servant's bed room. The door and table were charred by the attempt to set the girl's clothes on fire.

Drawing made of the foot of the stairs where the body of Rose was discovered by her father.

Photograph of
William Gardiner,
circa 1902.

MR
HENRY
ROUSE

Artist's sketch
of Henry Rouse,
agricultural labourer
and preacher.

D R

I will try to see you tonight at 12 oclock at your Place if you Put a light in your window at 10 oclock for about 10 minutes then you can take it out again. dont have a light in your Room at 12 as I will come round to the back

The assignation note that requested that Rose should place a light in her window for 10 minutes at 10 pm.

The only surviving picture of Rose Anne Harsent.

Above: The Doctors Chapel, scene of the meeting between Rose Harsent and William Gardiner and the revelation overheard by Wright and Skinner that started the scandal.

Below: Providence House, Peasenhall. The bedroom window of Rose's room is seen at top while the bedroom of the Crisps' bedroom is located below.

Mr Harsent, father of Rose who discovered his daughter's slain body at the foot of the kitchen stairs in Providence House.

Gamekeeper James Morris, who discovered the footprints leading to and away from Providence House.

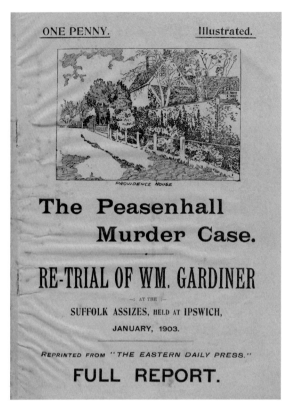

ONE PENNY.   Illustrated.

PROVIDENCE HOUSE

The Peasenhall Murder Case.

RE-TRIAL OF WM. GARDINER

— AT THE —

SUFFOLK ASSIZES, HELD AT IPSWICH,

JANUARY, 1903.

REPRINTED FROM "THE EASTERN DAILY PRESS."

FULL REPORT.

Front page newspaper headline of the impending second trial of William Gardiner.

Georgianna Gardiner, wife of William as depicted in a sketch.

The prosecution team of Mr Dickens and Mr Ridley eventually had to settle upon an architect who backed up Superintendent Andrews' account that there was no conclusive proof that neither Wright or Skinner could have heard Rose and Gardiner talking clearly due to the acoustics of the building and placement of the two aforementioned outside the building and two prison guards who would be used in the backing of letters sent by Gardiner from prison.

The judge presiding over the new trial was Mr Justice Lawrence and Mr Dickens opened the proceedings by explaining his idea of the murderer removing his shoes so as to not step in the copious amounts of blood, even though this wouldn't mean no footprints were left, he criticized the fact that the police had thought (under the guidance of Dr Lay) that it was a suicide from Sunday until Tuesday. He even had time to make known Mr Wild's previous mocking statement in the first trial when he said something along the lines that the tightly jammed cork in the medicine bottle would require the murderer to ask Rose for a corkscrew to get the paraffin out to burn her body. Mr Dickens put forward his own explanation for the cork in the bottle:

> For that purpose, we suggest, he took with him the bottle filled with paraffin oil, but in putting the cork in, with a view of putting it in in such a way that it was not likely to come out, he put it in so tightly that when the murderer took the bottle from his pocket he could not move the cork.

An admission was also made for the first time that the prosecution could not give a definitive time of death. The first witness called by the prosecution was the architect, Mr W.H. Brown. His findings of Providence House were given and under cross-examination from Mr Wild, Wild gave his own thoughts on the scene, as he was now familiar with the location's layout. It was a rather pointless witness choice that, in reality, achieved absolutely nothing for the prosecution.

Bill Wright appeared again and kept to his original testimony and Mr Wild quickly found that the new judge, Sir John Compton Lawrence, was not one to tolerate witty or lively remarks that would cause laughter in the courtroom. Mr Wild mentioned the statement previously made by Gardiner about the possible reasoning for Wright's anger towards him by being reprimanded by Mr Smyth over some poorly executed work. After that first trial, Mr Wild had obtained the reports from Smyths of reprimands for bad work. It was soon discovered that the 'telling off' had actually occurred a few weeks after the Doctor's Chapel debacle. Mr Wild therefore had to try and establish a previous incident:

Wild	Were you found at fault with your work?
Wright	No, not by Mr Smyth.
Wild	Mr Gardiner?
Wright	No, I don't think I was.
Wild	You don't know one way or the other?
Wright	I feel perfectly sure.
Wild	You feel a little surer as you go on? (laughter)
Judge	If there is anything like laughter, I will have the gallery cleared. People must remember what it is at which they are present.

Mr Justice Lawrence had instantly set the tone of his tolerance for sarcasm and Mr Wild refrained instantly. It was now that Wright took the upper hand against Mr Wild, as can be seen by the following exchange:

Wild	Did you leave out about hearing Rose Harsent say 'oh, oh!' and hearing the rustling noise?
Wright	Yes, I left that out.
Wild	Why?
Wright	Because it did not come into my mind; there was a long time between.

Wild	But there is a longer time between now?
Wright	I have been over it since.
Wild	Oh! Who have you been over it with?
Wright	I have with you.

A clearly witted response that was met with no laughter from the gallery – they had heeded Mr Justice Lawrence too. The one and only newly discovered fact from both Wright and Skinner was that when Gardiner had called for them he had indeed tried to deny ever being at the Doctor's Chapel that evening.

As mentioned before, the defence had visited the area in person to gather local gossip and the next person to take to the stand, Mr Henry Rouse, was to be the first to hear of what they had found out. Poor Mr Rouse was barraged with an onslaught of accusations from the loose-lipped villagers. He had apparently put out information against a local lad called Turrell whom he had accused of setting a barn alight at Wrentham; the local magistrates had eventually dismissed the case.

He was also accused of having an affair with the wife of a horse handler he had employed called Gooch. It was alleged that while Gooch was away on business, Rouse would go over to his cottage to see his wife. His defence of this accusation? Mr Gooch had become 'a God-fearing man', and it was nothing but pure coincidence that he happened to go to the house when Mr Gooch was out. Rouse also denied that he misbehaved with a lady whose name started with a B. It was beginning to look like Mr Rouse was Suffolk's equivalent of Casanova; not an ideal look for another man of God. The situation didn't improve for the poor Mr Rouse. He had apparently given evidence in a murder trial in 1884 when Edna Carter had suffocated her 2-year-old child in some woods near Wrentham. Rouse had apparently heard the child's cries whilst working nearby and had gone to investigate. Wild said Rouse had gladly put himself forward for the subsequent trial at Assizes court but Rouse insisted he only appeared before Halesworth magistrates. He was accused of trying to set individuals up into stealing and he'd tried to get a Miss Walker to back him up regarding reportedly seeing Gardiner put his feet in Rose's lap. Mr Wild even accused him of delivering his responses in the way he would deliver a sermon. Rouse left the box virtually destroyed. The jurors would surely discredit everything he had previously said now that he was demonstrated to be a somewhat doubtful character.

Rose's younger brother, Harry, did little to help the defence. He claimed he'd taken one or two letters from Gardiner to Rose in 1901 and another one or two in 1902. Under cross-examination Harsent contradicted himself and so his testimony was of little use.

Mrs Crisp was called again and, as before, continued with her nervous laughter as she replied to questioning. Mr Wild again rebuked her for it, 'You seem to think it is a great joke'.

'I am not joking, Mr Wild', she replied, 'Would you mind not addressing me by name?'

'Just answer the questions, please'. Mrs Crisp turned to the judge, 'My Lord, Mr Wild and Mr Leighton came to my house three weeks ago.' She then addressed Mr Wild, 'I have given you every opportunity to come to our house, and I do not know why you should doubt my word'. Understandably, she was not familiar with court proceedings and had obviously believed that upon their visit to her at Peasenhall they had struck up a relationship of a friendly nature that had now turned decidedly frosty. She clearly believed that inviting Mr Wild to her home and answering his questions should be deemed as her part in the case done and dusted.

Day two began with a smaller public attendance in the gallery. As in the previous trial, Harry Burgess and Mrs Dickinson testified again to their original stories, James Morris was picked up by the defence on the fact he had gone to look for footprints on the Sunday at midday but was unable to locate them, this was denied.

Herbert Stammers spoke of the large fire early on Sunday morning and William Harsent was to retell the story of how he found his daughter but, in unusual circumstances for a cross-examination, Mr Wild decided to save Mr Harsent the trauma of re-living the scene word by word, instead directing Mr Dickens to ask Mr Harsent direct questions about that morning, rather than having to go through it all again. So far nothing exceptional had been heard in evidence and once more it felt like the trial was going through the same laborious judicial motions; until, that is, Superintendent Staunton gave new evidence.

Mr Wild asked if Staunton had made inquiries at the Triple Plea public house located some eight miles from Peasenhall, where a traveller had stopped for breakfast on Sunday, 1 June 1902 after claiming to have walked from Peasenhall. He had done so but the traveller had by then moved on to Halesworth first and then moved on again and was lost and wasn't able to be questioned.

More shockingly though was the news that a letter of confession had been delivered to the *East Anglian Daily Times*. Mr Dickens became enraged and snapped back instantly but Mr Wild relayed that he fully intended to have the handwriting analysed.

In total three letters were found to be in existence. One at Ipswich, another surprisingly found in a lane in Devon, about as far west as you can go from Peasenhall, and the final letter was sent directly to PC Nunn. The judge said that if one was to be read aloud, all three must also be read, no matter how irrelevant they appeared to be. The letter to the *East Anglian Daily Times* was littered with misspelling and a lack of punctuation; it also contained three indecent phrases that were omitted in the courtroom.

From My darling Rose Ann Harsent('s) devoted true lover(.) but she was deceived me God only [K]no[ws] both with Gardiner and Davis[.] God only knows as Davis was the father off [sic] her child as my own darling Rose told me the night before committed this horrowble [sic] murder[.] but i hope she is at rest[.] bless her[!] but i feel i cannot rest night nor day as she is haunting me every night & every min[u]te [.] but

God is the farther of them both now [.] and i shall sertinly [sic] swing for that – Davice [Davis] for deceiving me as i [k]no[w] she was not so (pregnant) by me[.] and now i must confess as G[ardiner] is not the murder[er] of my darling rose as i am[.] but i am not a superer [?] nor a counter jumper but i am a mal[t]ster chap and have a mother to keep[.] but sir i must confess as i am told sharp for you all[.] you ar[e] all deleribily [sic] Liers about g(ardiner) we[a]ring barred glossours they was my malting shoes with barres across and i must confess that i filled both shoes full of stones as they was all blood[.] and tied a brick and but them in the water so as no traces could you get on them[.] and i must confess that i had them on and went from Peasenhall in my old malted shoes Crisp['s] house so as you would think G[ardiner] had done it but he is incionint [sic] as Mr Justice Grantham[.] i am laughing in my sleeves to think you can not find me[.] there is t[w]o of us who was there and B was watching while i did it[.] my darling rose gave me 5£ for a last token[.] i am sorrow for for [sic] poor Dad now[.] as for old woman crisp she is nothing but a nasty-lier and that is swe[a]ring to say that she came down at 12 o'clock[.] she did not as i was in the house at the time[.] and i did write the letter to my pet lamb to tell her to put the light in the window for me as it was not the first time i had been there at that time[.] as i can go so far as to say i have had my darling in my arms all night (words omitted) and was on the sofer [sic] the night i did the murder[.] but i can swe[a]r as rose told me she had been unfaithful to me with D[avis] and if a man can stand that[.] tell me[,] all through (although?) we was on the rug to Gether befor [sic] i killed her[.] and as for the medesin [sic] bottle rose gave me some whiskey in it the night before and i took the paraffin in it from my own home at suffolk[.] and you must fined [sic] out the rest as i have been had (at?) malting to day and i cannot send you my name but shall committe sueside [sic] before long[.] when we come back we shall put old crisp and his old woman through the mill worse than my rose[.] and as for her (mrs crisp) saying she heard a noise she did not as i filled her (Rose's) mouth full of my muffler as i did (it) in a cool blood[.] not hot[,] as i know she would be deceiving me this (malting) season while i was away like last[,] but it was Harsent that said my only Love had been unfaithful to me by going with Gardiner[.] and now i must confess that no one will act immorall [sic] with her again as (words omitted) before i killed her[.] and G[ardiner] must thank God they was not served the same fate[.] but they will do even my trou[s]e[r]s and shirt was drowned (thrown in water?) with brick end inside them[.] but [i] shall not say w[h]ere[.] find out[.] i have to take lodnum [laudanum] to inset [sic] sleep as i cannot rest without my own darling pet[.] had i not have took all my letters out of rose's box i should be w[h]ere g(ardiner) is and had the rope now[.] but go on[.] let g(ardiner) have it[.] or else D(avis) he is the corse [sic] of this[.] he is been the ruin of my young life[.] and now, must conclude by saying it will be a good job alone with. From H B the murder[er] of my own darling lover[.] i could not think of her having (words omitted) by that - Davis[.] i shall put a bullet straight through them as i shall be coming back in six months[.] now i am a murderer.

Reading the letter above may remind readers of the infamous Jack the Ripper hoax letters that flooded in during the Whitechapel Murders some fourteen years prior to Rose's death. Similar to those letters, this one is also littered with terrible spelling and grammar, which is probably an indication of the education levels of the working class at the time, and basically said nothing at all that was not already publicly known as the case had been extensively covered by the local paper, *The East Anglian Daily Times*.

The case had also made the national daily papers of the time too. It made for a perfect scandal and murder mystery for the people of the time; a generation that had been brought up on Sherlock Holmes and stories by Edgar Allan Poe. Mr Wild saw potential in it, it was well informed, he said, and that the author had faked his illiteracy, but most importantly he thought the handwriting itself was similar to the assignation letters but there was some element that could not be ignored – the letter was posted in Burton upon Trent on 1 December 1902. Oddly, a migration of Suffolk workers had seasonally travelled to work in Burton at Bass, the brewing company, since 1879. This was the ideal basis for Mr Wild to cast the net to find the murderer to be from much farther away, and it certainly would have made the jurors think much harder about the guilty party. It must be said though that the Suffolk-based workforce often included young lads from Peasenhall itself, and that could very easily explain how the author knew so much about the circumstances he wrote of. In truth it was discovered to be nothing more than an individual playing a sick joke. The other letters followed as evidence but it was clear that they were just nothing more than a clear hoax and not worthy of consideration because of the clear inconsistencies that were contained within them.

Dr Richardson appeared next along with Dr Lay and Dr Stevenson. A juror enquired if he believed Rose had been standing when she was murdered but he was absolutely certain she had been laying down as the way her throat was cut meant the murderer was to her right side because the wounds inflicted would have been hard to perform so cleanly if Rose had been standing. This would explain why the blood was on her left side, though he did speculate that she had been stabbed at least once while she stood.

Now, back to the letter from the anonymous author from Burton. It is clear that the three parts omitted in court were in reference to the act of sexual intercourse taking place. Mr Justice Lawrence asked Dr Richardson if this had indeed likely occurred. Dr Richardson said that he did have a suspicion that intercourse had happened prior to the murder, but that he was not in a position to swear that it had taken place. This is deeply problematic because had the police and medical examiners had the benefit of today's technology it would have been a case closed situation one way or the other. It is ironic that in June 1902 the very first criminal to be convicted of a crime through fingerprint identification, Harry Jackson, after he stole some billiard balls in a burglary that occurred in Denmark Hill, London. Handwriting technology was performed by an expert who worked on the police force but at the time it was not an exact science and often cases were not concluded with this evidence, unlike today where, thanks to the invention of computers, the accuracy of writing examples is now considered to be 98 per cent accurate. The fact this letter was written on 1 December 1902 when William Gardiner was tucked safely behind bars in Ipswich means that either the author of the letter was playing a cruel prank to waste police time or he was indeed the murderer and Gardiner was completely innocent. It was certainly food for thought for the jury. In later years, a photographer who had been at the crime scene, Alderman F. Jenkins, spoke of the sight he had witnessed in the kitchen and, to his mind, there was absolutely no doubt that Rose had had sexual intercourse that night with her murderer due to the fact she was wearing just her nightdress with no undergarments beneath. Sadly this important information was never followed through on but could have been very conclusive if Rose had been tested for semen traces when she was discovered.

Next into the witness box was poor Frederick Davis. He had been the author of the saucy letters and poems Rose had supposedly asked him to provide her. In the first trial he was torn apart by the defence counsel and Mr Wild was equally harsh on him the second time around. Mr Wild was still adamant that Davis was the father of Rose's unborn child but Davis vehemently denied it again. The courtroom notes list an exchange between counsels at this point:

Dickens	I presume my friend, Mr Wild, takes the same line as before, and does not suggest Davis had any part in the murder.
Wild	I know nothing about it.
Dickens	You said in the terms that you did not impute it to him in the slightest degree!
Wild	I should not be so wicked as to make any such suggestion.

To conclude the days' proceedings, the subject of the assignation letter was brought up. Mr Gurrin still believed the letter had not been written in disguised writing but had been written with due care, however the envelope, he said, had been disguised. He concluded (quite obviously) that the letter from Burton upon Trent was not written in Gardiner's hand and with this the court was closed for the day.

As day two began, Mr Dickens called prison warden John Shepard. He was to confirm a letter had been written by Gardiner to his solicitor whilst in prison. This letter apparently resembled the writing within the assignation letter quite closely. Other than this, both counsels had nothing new to offer the jury and it was a case of going over everything again as a part of the closing statements. Mr Wild concentrated on Mrs Crisp's haphazard recollection of the times she reported hearing the scream and thud and he insinuated that this was because police timing of the events had persuaded her to rethink her statements. He went on to squash Mr Stammer's story of the 'great fire' he'd observed early on 1 June saying that if Gardiner had been burning clothes or rubber shoes he would have smelt it before seeing it and also that upon police inspection, no trace of the burning of these items was found. As for the medicine bottle, Mr Wild couldn't resist his sarcastic approach by saying:

But for (the bottle) Gardiner would never have been accused in this case. But the police in Peasenhall had got the bottle, and they said to themselves: 'Gardiner did this murder, and he has left his card. Out of consideration for us, in order not to tax our brains too heavily, Gardiner has considerately brought a labelled bottle with his name on it – and, of course, he did the murder.' If this were not a murder case, it would make us laugh.

This was a tricky subject to address but a vital one which needed to be answered. Mr Wild knew that this was crucial to the prosecution because who but the killer would know that a medicine bottle that was kept at the house would contain paraffin? Wouldn't it make sense that the bottle was pre-filled by the murderer himself as he fully intended to try and burn the body? Mr Wild continued…

In all probability the bottle was on that shelf which was broken, because you remember the shelf was standing above the side of the door and the bottle fell down, and the pieces were found just on the left of the girl's head. It would be exactly where they would be found if they fell off the shelf. The very fact of this paraffin falling in the scuffle that must have ensued made the (murderer) suddenly think: 'I will try to burn the body,' so he at once went to get the paraffin out of her lamp, and in his hurry neglected to hide the bottle.

Mr Wild was to deliver his thoughts for two and a half hours. Unsurprisingly after such a long time speaking, Mr Wild left the courtroom to rest so it was left to his junior, Claughton Scott, to ask Dr Elliston about the wounds to Rose's throat . Dr Elliston had not viewed Rose and so passed over the question. Georgianna Gardiner appeared next but, again, had nothing to offer the defence and appeared so ill that she required the use of smelling salts to get through the ordeal. As the court adjourned for lunch she promptly fainted. She was not called for cross-examination after lunch and remained in an hysterical state for several hours.

It was now the turn of Gardiner to take the stand once again. He stood strong and answered the questions put to him in a determined manner but offered nothing new to the courtroom.

Mrs Pepper similarly appeared with nothing new, Mrs Walker admitted Rose had received camphorated oil to aid her cold from Mrs Gardiner and also said that her daughter Eve had never seen Gardiner act improperly at chapel. Nothing further was added and court was adjourned until the next day.

Day three began and Mr Dickens had a chance to cross-examine Mrs Gardiner. No chance was taken and a doctor was at hand should she suffer one of her 'turns'. Thankfully, she made it through unscathed. Mr Wild began summing up. He now tried the approach of pulling at the jurors' heart strings, even leaving Gardiner in floods of tears in the dock. He invited the jury to cross reference the assignation letter with the samples of Gardiner's writing and even said that if they believed Gardiner guilty then his wife would have had a part to play in it also. This of course is true. There simply could be no way a married man could hide such a crime from his wife. Mr Wild finished with a real tear-jerker by saying, 'Gentleman, pretty well the last thing the poor man did before he was locked up for eight months was to be in bed with his little infant; and the child worked its way, nestled up to its father – that father whom you are asked to say is a murderer – and the wife noticed the arm around the little girl.

Touching stuff indeed, and Gardiner for the third time that day sobbed loudly in the dock. The prosecution now had their say. Mr Dickens was less emotional in his address, unsurprisingly. He argued that Gardiner was indeed popular in Peasenhall and no witness against him had any malice and no reason to single him out for persecution.

It was now time for Mr Justice Lawrence to sum up to the jury. Unlike Mr Justice Grantham in the first trial, he was lighter with his words and didn't make it sound as though the defence may well have not bothered turning up. He did make errors though; his first was to say 'it is said there had been a scandal about this girl and him, and that there had been reports before the scandal on May 1st'.

Both counsels instantly stood up with Wild exclaiming, 'My Lord, I don't think there were any reports before the Chapel incident.' 'I have looked at my notes,' retorted the judge, 'and am very careful about it; I can prove to you both, if necessary, that there had been.' No matter his protestations he was indeed wrong but no further challenge was put to him.

The next blooper came by the way of the Methodist statements:

'These gentlemen come here to contradict Mr Guy, and to contradict each other. I am bound to say, in an important matter, for some said Mr Guy said he would rather believe two in the church than two out – and that does not show a very judicial spirit - whilst two said he said it was a fabrication of lies'. This again had not been the case as the Methodist witnesses didn't contradict each other at any time. Towards the end he made an apparent anti-Gardiner statement.

> Whether he is the father of the child or not does not so much matter. It appears to me that the matter of importance is whether he was having immoral relations with the girl... [H]ere is a man who knew this girl was six months enceinte, and had had immoral relations with her for a considerable time, and who, whether he was the father or not, was pretty sure to have the credit of being the father. You have been rightly told...That if you have a reasonable doubt, the accused is entitled to the benefit of it. But the doubt in a case of this kind must be fair and reasonable and not a trivial doubt, such as the speculative ingenuity of counsel might suggest.

With this he sent the jury away to consider their verdict; they returned just two hours and fifteen minutes later unable to reach a conclusive verdict.

Unbelievably, this set of jurors couldn't decide in full agreement and word has it that this time the result was the opposite to the verdict of the first trial, but even so, once more one person had saved Gardiner from the gallows. There would have to be a third trial at a new venue – Bury St Edmunds – in six months' time.

Chapter Seven

After the Second Trial

Upon hearing the verdict Gardiner was greatly demoralised, he was sure that the scales of justice would tip against him this time. He was unbalanced upon leaving the dock to be taken back to his cell. By the time of the next trial he would have already served a little more than a year in jail with a potential death sentence hanging over him. The national papers relayed the news the following day, it had now became a case that was of national interest. The papers in their comments on the case were universal in condemning the judicial service and pure injustice of leaving Gardiner to fester in jail for six more months. It appeared that public opinion was now fully in Gardiner's favour. As before, the *East Anglian Daily Times* opened a fund for Gardiner. The first donation was of £20 by Mr Evan Edwards again and within a week £67 was raised, equivalent to £8,680 in today's money.

Following the closure of the trial, Georgianna planned to return home to Peasenhall from her sister's house in Ipswich and to have all her children around her after the weeks she'd been away. On Wednesday, 28 January, she attempted to visit her husband only to have her cab mobbed after leaving the front door. She was in emotional turmoil and completely spent by the ordeal and six more months of torture would surely come at a big price to her. In the meantime, *The Sun* newspaper in London (not the same publication as today's newspaper that bears the same name) started a petition to have Gardiner released and also a shilling fund. The petition gathered over 6,000 signatures in two days and it is uncertain how much the shilling fund raised.

On Thursday Georgianna finally arrived home to her children and was met with cold, hard stares. The general populace may have leaned towards Gardiner's innocence, but the residents of Peasenhall had long ago made up their minds that Gardiner was guilty, indeed the church hierarchy, who once were on Gardiner's side, must themselves have even doubted their initial innocent verdict at the affair. Georgianna retreated to her cottage and closed the door, leaving all the turmoil outside the confines of her home. *The Sun* however, in London, was printing a special edition with a bold prediction – William Gardiner would be soon released under a *noue prosequi*, a legal Latin term meaning 'to be unwilling to pursue' or, in more general terms, there would be no point continuing the case because of the costs to the taxpayer and the fact no further evidence to swing the jury in the direction of a guilty verdict could be found. The prediction came true the following morning; it was revealed that Gardiner had been released at 8.30pm the previous evening. Apparently when told of his imminent release Gardiner simply replied, 'I always knew I should be acquitted'. This, of course, was not true. He hadn't been acquitted at all; it was quite simply that it would prove too costly to send him for trial again and, as it was becoming ever clearer that public opinion was in his favour, could a completely unbiased jury be summoned to try his case? The answer in all likelihood was a resounding 'no'. Gardiner was met at the prison by Mr Leighton and his assistant, Horace Bullen, and was taken away by cab to a house where he undertook a makeover, having his substantial beard shaved off, leaving just a thick moustache (a popular fashion for the period). It was a look he was to keep for the rest of his life. In an exclusive interview for the *East Anglian Daily Times* (they had after all supported him and his family generously since the previous year's first trial) he said:

> I don't know how to thank the paper for what it has done. Had it not been for the fund you started, my defence at the second trial could not have been conducted with such vigour as it was

by Mr Wild. I am heartily thankful to you and all the papers that have taken up my case.

Unsurprisingly, Rose was mentioned, to which Gardiner said:

> Well, she was really more of a friend of my wife's than mine, she used to do little odd sewing jobs for my wife, and I was so occupied at my cottage on the night of the murder, I didn't see her that night, though as she was gone when I returned home…. My relationship with the girl was only as a friend at the chapel.

The publicity for Gardiner was immense; he was offered a chance to earn £20 a week for a six-month run in theatres. Gardiner turned this down, seeking to return home, but what he didn't realise is that he could not return to Peasenhall due to the hostilities towards him and his family. It was then decided that Gardiner should go to London to evade further public and press interference. Georgianna found out the news of her husband's release via a letter at 7pm on the day of his release and became overcome with emotion and couldn't leave her room for some hours before travelling to Darsham with Mr Batten where she caught a train back to Ipswich. She was met by Mr Leighton who took her to his office for yet another interview with the *East Anglian Daily Times* and didn't seem to agree that they should move from Peasenhall because as far as she was concerned her husband now had nothing to prove.

As can be expected, the inhabitants of Peasenhall were not as happy about Gardiner's release and *noue prosequi* verdict. They didn't want him to return at any cost, they had long ago decided that he was guilty and should have been hanged. Scandal arose when knowledge of Gardiner's weekly wage paid by Mr Smyth, Gardiner's old boss – just twenty-six shilling a week – and Mr Smyth begged the *East Anglian Daily Times* not to forget to mention he actually took home thirty-six shillings due to work premiums. Smyth made the point known about the wages because it was known that he underpaid his workforce compared to similar jobs around the country. He wouldn't say if he'd take Gardiner back. He knew if he did it was highly likely his entire workforce would walk out. Luckily he had covered his bases because he had initially only held Gardiner's job open for three months during the first trial and had since filled the position. For those who like a spooky coincidence, the man who replaced William Gardiner in his job was also named William Gardiner (no relation) and when the original Gardiner left his cottage when the family moved to London, the new family of Gardiners moved into Alma cottage – you really couldn't make this up.

Back to London, where Gardiner gave more interviews to newspapers. First the *Daily Express,* then *The Star,* where he said 'on the evidence of Mrs Crisp and Mrs Dickinson nobody could have convicted me', and continued…

> The explanation is that a very bad murder was committed there, that nobody knew who it was, and when the Police said they had got the man, most of the villagers accepted the situation. There would have been just the same feeling against any other man the Police charged with the murder. But you must remember, also that a foreman can never be very popular if he does his duty…

> I was never a man to go to the public house or in that class of society where a man becomes popular, but those who know me – the thinking part of the people – believed in me and do so still. I had worked my way up from the bottom of the

ladder, and there were several men there who had been there years before me, and when I was made foreman that caused jealousy. Then I went to Paris for the firm, and that made things worse.

In early February, another problem in Peasenhall became apparent; it looked like the post addressed to the Gardiners was going missing, and so a trap was set up by a Mr Green, the postmaster at Yoxford, and a Mr Frederick Mann, a detective clerk sent by the general post office. They marked two letters addressed to Georgianna with a dot made by pencil on the envelope corner and counted the nine items of mail for delivery to her. The letters were given to Brewer for delivery, he gave them to sub-postmaster Hurren and his daughter Christianna; the letters included seven for Georgianna and one for Ettie. When Brewer returned to the post office, the only letter there was one for Ettie.

With foul play confirmed, Messers Green and Mann despatched to Peasenhall to confront the sub-postmaster, taking police inspector Fowler with them. Upon arriving they found Christianna, his daughter, who said she knew nothing of it when confronted. Mann stated the letters had been posted and so a full search would need to be carried out. Instantly, she produced seven letters for Mrs Gardiner, all of which had been opened but their contents remained.

Christianna was cautioned because another thirty-nine letters for the Gardiners were missing. She led them upstairs where thirty-eight of those were recovered, of which thirty-six contained postal orders adding up to almost £10 (£1,230 in today's money). Luckily for her there was no evidence of an attempt to cash them but an explanation was certainly needed. Her answer was blunt and very much to the point: 'I had a mind to look into them. I have had a lot of trouble over Gardiner, Sundays and all. He does not deserve the money. He ought to be hung. The post office doesn't pay us too much money'.

Miss Hurren was obviously a very bitter woman but some could sympathise with her in a way. She worked hard seven days a week for next to no money and here was a man getting money for nothing, not to mention – in her mind at least – a murderer. The post office had no option but to prosecute her for tampering with the mail, which is a serious offence even today. She appeared before magistrates and pleaded guilty. She was lucky and given a conditional discharge.

And with that final mystery solved, the Peasenhall murder scandal would come to an end as far as the general population was concerned but, in the tiny community of Peasenhall, the murder was hard to forget. The main characters of the investigation did try to move on though and here is what is known of their lives following the case:

Bill Wright: Collapsed and died in the road in 1904 of kidney trouble and dropsy.

Henry Rouse: Died of rheumatic arthritis in 1905.

Harry Harsent: Died in 1906 of inflammation of the lungs.

William Harsent: Died in 1910.

Alfonso Skinner: Died in 1960 near Basingstoke.

Fred Davis: Worked at a furniture store near Luton, married in 1910 and passed away in 1965.

Ernest Wild: Was knighted in the 1918 King's Birthday Honours. He retired from parliament at the 1922 general election and was appointed Recorder of London, the senior presiding judge at the central criminal court at the Old Bailey in London. He died on 13 September 1934, aged 65.

Henry Fielding Dickens: Continued his legal work and was appointed Knight Bachelor in 1922. He retired in 1932 and was to pass away one year later in 1933, five days after being hit by a motorcycle while crossing Chelsea Embankment. He was 84 years old and the last living child of his famous father, Charles Dickens.

George Andrews: Went on to retire in 1931 and received the traditional gold watch.

Eli Nunn: Passed away in 1931.

George Staunton: Made his way through the ranks of the Suffolk Constabulary and became chief constable in 1933.

Frederick Brewer: Retired from postal duties in 1924.

After the trial, the Gardiners moved away to Brentford in Essex, although the press reported the family had moved to the north of England. They eventually bought a shop which was simply called, 'Gardiner'. It was a combination of a traditional store, confectionist and tobacconist, at 63 Hartington Road, Southall Green, Norwood. They had two more children and William spent his time between the shop and employment at A&B Hansen, builders and undertakers, where his carpentry skills came in very handy. He still led an upstanding and moral life but fully detached himself from the Methodist Church.

An interesting side note to the Gardiners' stay in London is that the people there who knew them said Georgianna was the stronger willed of the two and very possessive, while William was much more reserved – the complete opposite to the opinions of those living in Peasenhall. Had the trials played their part in this change? Perhaps Gardiner was deeply affected by his ordeal and had become greatly humbled (and thankful) that he'd escaped the hangman's noose and had lived to see another day. As for Georgianna, perhaps the ordeal had strengthened her character from that of a wilting violet to a woman cast in stone? Let us not forget that at the trials, she was prone to bouts of hysterics and fainting at just the thought of giving evidence and being cross-examined. The question must also be asked, was Georgianna just a very convincing actor in the courtroom?

She was also known to her London neighbours to be very kind and would openly offer advice to anyone with troubles and even befriended a girl there who was similar to Rose. And even stated when asked about the Peasenhall scandal that it was 'the man's fault'.

William Gardiner was to eventually pass away in 1941 aged seventy-four in hospital. Before his death he was said to have vociferously sung hymns like a man half his age would have. His final words were to be 'It is over'. Georgianna survived him by seven years and in that time she continued to run the shop with her daughter.

Chapter Eight

Case Summary and Conclusion

Many criminologists today believe that this was a straightforward case: William Gardiner killed Rose Harsent and he quite literally got away with murder but is there any possibility that there could have been another responsible for this horrendous crime?

One theory is that perhaps Georgianna had something to do with it. It is without doubt that she would have been greatly affected by the accusations surrounding her husband and Rose and one can only imagine what had gone through her head over the course of that twelve-month period. She had also lost a child in this time frame and her mental state must have been in absolute turmoil. She was a proud woman and, as we learned from people who knew her in London, was a strong force who was believed to be the stronger of the couple, a complete reversal of what the people of Peasenhall had said of her character. Something had changed, so which Georgianna was the 'real' Georgianna?

Without doubt she was a devoted wife and mother and would, almost certainly, also have done anything to maintain the status quo of her family. Just exactly when she learned of the scandal no one will ever know but what is clear is that she stuck by her husband resolutely throughout and even provided an alibi for him later in a well rehearsed story by later saying her husband was with her during the storm and also saying her husband did not light the fire at the time reported on the Sunday morning. But the question remains: could she have slipped away to commit the murder, with her husband actually covering for

Georgianna, whilst covering his own back, and would she have been capable of the crime?

Physically speaking, she most definitely would have been capable of the murder as both women were of equal size and that, combined with the element of surprise, would have given her the upper hand in the attack. She would have access to the medicine bottle for sure, seemingly knowing more about the bottle than her husband, and therefore could quite easily place the paraffin within reach before grabbing a copy of the *East Anglian Daily Times* and making her way to Providence House; but is there really a motive here for murder? Sure, murders have been committed over less and it is true that a high percentage of murders involve jilted lovers but would Georgianna fall into this category? I believe that she at no time showed any sign of a temperament capable of murder, and even playing devil's advocate one could also say the very same of Gardiner himself. Clearly the scandal would have hurt her and made her ask many questions of herself, her husband and way of life. She would have wondered why her upstanding husband should seek a relationship with such a girl as Rose but I am sure that William would have dismissed this attraction to her as 'being the devil's work', a man of such strong religious beliefs must be at risk of being tempted by the devil himself, and what better way than him being led into temptation by a 'wicked girl'. This was still very much a time of strong religious beliefs and the power and word of God would dominate over all thoughts, actions and words of a mere mortal; if anything went wrong it was the devil and his hordes trying to claim more souls.

Of course, it is perfectly acceptable to suggest that both of the Gardiners were in this together and had conspired to commit and cover up the murder. Georgianna does seem to have given her husband an alibi on more than one occasion but was this through love for her husband and her thinking that he could not have committed such a horrendous crime or was it because she had committed the deed herself? Julian Fellowes of *Downton Abbey* fame made a documentary on the murder some years ago and his final conclusion was that Georgianna had committed the murder and that the case was that of a woman scorned taking out her revenge on the 'other woman'.

Many years after the murder, another rumour began circulating. A Mrs R.J. Meads of Southall, who was a school friend of the Gardiners' twin daughters, had relayed a story told to her and her husband that members of the Gardiner family actually believed Georgianna had committed the murder. The story goes that Georgianna was pregnant herself at the time of the murder, subsequently losing the child during the ordeal of the trials. She also said many other things that were not true and unproved so this can readily be dismissed out of hand. One thing that was definite about the crime scene was the footprints leading to and from it were unquestionably those of a man.

So, if we rule Georgianna out due to the evidence of the footprints, can we find any other culprit?

We should perhaps look at Rose's 'fiancé', Bob Kerridge. He seems to have been an elusive character throughout the case, with nothing of note being recorded of him, despite his seemingly close relationship with the victim. It should be noted that it is believed that the Doctor's Chapel incident resulted in him breaking off his engagement with Rose but perhaps he didn't? Could this man be fully responsible for arranging that fateful meeting and, in a blind rage killing Rose before slipping away into the night? He had swiftly moved to Uggeshall after the murder and remained away over the course of the trials before eventually returning to Peasenhall when the dust had cleared.

It seemed the people of Peasenhall held him close to their hearts though as nobody ever spoke badly of him. He went on to become a Methodist preacher in later life after spending his working life as a farm labourer. In 1905 he married Frances Lizzie Hunt and this may have set back his advancement within the church as it delayed him getting qualifications to become a preacher which he began within the year of the murder. It was noted that he was taking longer to complete the homework needed to fulfill the role and it was suggested he should return the books if he was not interested in the position. He eventually completed the work though and initially became the chapel trustee.

He was clearly a man devoted to the church and the testimonies of the locals about his character make it seem, from the outside, highly unlikely that he would have committed the murder. He later went on to become a sexton at Sibton and, after his wife passed away, he remarried to a woman who, by all accounts, didn't care for him as his first wife had. He died in 1957 and was greatly missed within the community, with no one having an ill word of him. It makes one wonder quite why young Rose should have become involved with another when she was engaged to a man such as Bob.

In Rose Harsent's story, there is only one other man to be mentioned, Frederick Davis. We have seen how Mr Wild believed him to be the culprit simply because after examining her correspondence, Davis' letters implied his affection for her and suggested he wanted a more intimate relationship. Did this pairing come to fruition, leading to Rose's pregnancy? It is true that Mr and Mrs Gardiner said that he had been out with Rose and it appears that she had obtained a pamphlet on contraception from him in late 1901. The Gardiners may have been using him as a scapegoat to take the heat away from William. It must be remembered that Davis would have had to pass two sleeping people to get out of his lodgings – his brother and father, who remained undisturbed that night – but also that he had no person who could verify his movements either. Research has since uncovered that Davis did have a temperamental side; in early 1902 he appeared at Halesworth Petty Sessions on 11 February and the local paper noted the following report of the case:

> Frederick Davis and Harry Smith were charged with assaulting
> Alice Spoor, at Peasenhall, on the 19th of January. Mr A.H.
> Mullens appeared for the defendants. The prosecution said

she was out in the evening with her mother for a walk, and saw Harry Smith, who said her hat was not paid for, and threw stones at her. She had a stick in her hand and went to hit Smith with it.

Davies came up and told Smith to let her have it. Davies smacked her head against the wall, seized her throat with his left hand. A lad named Lambert, came up and held her by the shoulder and Davies took the stick out of her hand and kept it. In cross-examination she admitted the stick was loaded with lead, but her mother did not have a stick, and she did not strike Smith, who went into an allotment and ran away, and she met him at another gate, but did not hit him, although she tried to do so. Mrs Spoor gave corroborative evidence, but contradicted herself and her daughter in cross-examination in several particulars. Mr Mullens for the defence said that the defendant (complainant) started all the trouble and Smith was standing in the street when the complainant's mother made a disgusting remark to him, and the complainant struck him with a loaded stick, and followed him and struck him again. Evidence in support of this statement was given by each of the defendants, and by Arthur Lambert. PC Eli Nunn gave defendants a good character, and the bench dismissed the case.

What can we make of this story? It is certainly very interesting to read of the violent behaviour of Davis. Of particular note is the fact that he 'smacked' the woman's head against a wall before placing his hand upon her throat; something that could have occurred during Rose's murder as she was hit first and then pushed against the door before she was stabbed and had her throat cut.

He certainly seemed to have an instinct to be over the top in such an innocent situation in his rush to defend his friend but it cannot be ignored that PC Eli Nunn spoke favourably of him and vouched for his usual good demeanour. It must be also remembered that the writing experts stated clearly that Davis's writing was not like that of the fateful note sent to Rose. If he'd have been investigated as a suspect for the murder, as William Gardiner had, would it have been found that young Fred Davis was completely innocent of any involvement in the murder based on a good reputation and the note alone? Gardiner also had a good reputation before the rumour scandal, and it couldn't be proved he wrote the note either.

Stewart P. Evans, former Suffolk police officer turned crime historian and author, composed a time chart of the events of 31 May – 1 June 1902 that was published in **The Peasenhall Murder** by Martin Fido and Keith Skinner, which, I believe, sums up the events perfectly. Reproduced with permission, it reads as follows:

9.00pm	Rose calls at Gardiners' back door. Family out.
9.30pm	Gardiner comes home. Children put to bed. Rose places light in the window, then goes downstairs.
9.55pm	Burgess sees Gardiner at the front door.
10.00pm	Burgess was seen chatting with Gardiner. Light seen in Providence House.
10.05pm	Storm brewing. Wind easterly.
10.10pm	Burgess leaves Gardiner.
10.15pm	Mrs Crisp sees Rose in the hall. (Rose sits on bed, waiting).
11.00pm	Thunder and heavy rain. Crisp goes downstairs.
11.30pm	Mrs Gardiner goes into Mrs Dickinson's. Rose goes into the kitchen.
12.00am	Rose in kitchen for assignation. The murderer arrives. Quarrel and murder. Mrs Crisp hears screams.
12.00am	Gardiner joins wife at Mrs Dickinson's.
12.30am	Gardiner testifies 'joined wife at 12.30' – a slip by Gardiner.
1.00am	Gardiner chatting with Mrs Dickinson.

1.30am	Storm abates; Mr Gardiner goes home, checks the children. Gardiner purports to visit privy? Gardiner starts a fire in Providence House?
2.00am	The Gardiners undress and go to bed. Mrs Gardiner cannot sleep.
2.20am	Bertie wakes up. Mrs Gardiner goes to him, Mrs Gardiner returns to bed. Gardiner is still in bed. Mrs Gardiner rises again for brandy.
3.00am	Dawn around this time.
3.30am	Twins wake up (time uncertain), Mrs Gardiner puts one with big sister. Brings other into bed with Gardiner.
4.00am	Hart passes along Hackney Road and Heveningham Long Lane.
5.00am	Mrs Gardiner falls asleep for the first time. Morris sees footprints.
6.30am	Gardiner lights a fire and burns clothes.
7.00am	Stammers sees fire.
7.30am	Stammers sees Gardiner coming away from the wash house.
8.00am	Gardiners get up. William Harsent finds body at Providence House.
8.30am	Gardiner makes fire for the kettle.
8.40am	PC Nunn arrives at scene of murder.

It has to be noted that when in court, Gardiner's entire defence rested on an awful lot of people being wrong or lying – Skinner and Wright about that night in the chapel, and when asked about his footprints to and from Providence House, how many shirts he owned or indeed why the medicine bottle should be at the scene, he could not supply an answer.

Stewart makes points that make perfect sense in his timeline. For example, the prosecution assumed that Gardiner planned to kill Rose and then burn all evidence of her body and the child but this is not usually how these cases work. Gardiner most likely had no intention of killing Rose that night but wanted merely to meet to suggest his solution to the problem. The problem most likely came in the shape of Rose not wishing to take Gardener up on his offer – possibly of relocation for Rose and her unborn child – and also that Gardiner was quick and ill-tempered by nature. Stewart says that Gardiner met Rose before an argument ensued and the murder was committed in the heat of the moment. He then went to Mrs Dickinson's before returning home where he made the excuse of using the privy whilst in fact returning the short distance to Providence House to attempt to start the fire. A piece of important information that was learned after the trial was that on 31 May 1902, the Peasenhall band had been performing in the town of Leiston, some 9 miles away, and as they returned to Peasenhall in the evening, Smyth's carriage was heard behind them with Gardiner driving it. Upon seeing the band he slowed down and then took a diversion via Rendham to return home. He obviously didn't want to be seen but he was, and his diversion was the reason for him returning so late on a non-work day. He had been to Leiston himself to try to secure lodgings for Rose and the soon-to-be-born child. This implies that he had no intention of killing Rose, just hide her away until the baby was born.

I propose that Gardiner wrote the assignation letter and disguised his handwriting purely to distance himself from Providence House and Rose so that after the birth of the child, should Rose decide she couldn't live in Leiston and wished to return to Peasenhall, it would be her word against his as to paternity. Who would people believe? An ill-educated servant girl or a fine upstanding hard working family man of God? The move was no doubt to allow Gardiner time to decide how to deal with the situation or perhaps so that Rose could give birth and then give the baby away before then returning to work. It is possible that Gardiner wanted to support Rose and their child but keep them out of the way. Regardless of the reason, upon seeing Rose at the agreed time on 31 May, Gardiner told her what had to be done but she disagreed with him – perhaps she didn't want to move away, perhaps suggesting Gardiner should leave his wife, or maybe he was washing his hands of the matter entirely – no financial support, nothing. They argued and, as Gardiner was quick tempered, he struck Rose out of anger and frustration on the cheek. He grabbed the knife from his pocket and stabbed her above the collar bone, she fell backwards onto the floor where Gardiner, in a blind panic and red mist rage, silenced her by cutting her throat. He then left the scene and this is the reason for why the timings differ.

William and Georgianna originally said that it was shortly after 11pm that they went to Mrs Dickinson's; that's what they told Staunton. Mrs Dickinson contradicted the time and gave the story of how William attended the children during the storm. This seems far from convincing as Gardiner wasn't the model parent type; remember, it was Georgianna who got up to the children twice in the night whilst Gardiner slept. The Gardiners tried to maintain they had gone to Mrs Dickinson within a few minutes of each other, but Mrs Dickinson was adamant there was a thirty-minute difference with Gardiner arriving closer to midnight. Gardiner let this slip himself, at trial:

Mr Wild	Do you remember what time you went to Mrs Dickinson's?
Gardiner	Half past twelve.
Mr Wild	Half past what?
Gardiner	Half past eleven, I mean.

Remembering that Rose's bed had not been slept in, only sat upon, shows she didn't have long to wait after the window was illuminated by candlelight at 10pm, so this fits in perfectly. So between 11.30pm and midnight the deed was done and this gave Gardiner the perfect opportunity to slip home, remove his blood-stained clothes before quickly changing and putting on his carpet slippers and then travelling the short distance to Mrs Dickinson's house. Imagine the turmoil now, sitting with company having just murdered the mother of your unborn child: had there been any evidence left behind? Any scrap of evidence would ultimately result in an appointment with the hangman's noose. Don't forget that in cases like this the husband/boyfriend/lover is always initially suspected by the police and PC Nunn instantly made this assumption too. Even in modern times this is the case; a recent survey conducted in 2020 showed that 47,000 women had been murdered by their partner or husband, this shocking statistic relates to one female death every 11 minutes. Had it not been for the original conclusion Dr Lay made that Rose had committed suicide, Gardiner would surely have been arrested straight away based on the previous rumours surrounding a potential affair. It was clear in Gardiner's mind – he had to start a fire to destroy all traces of evidence. But how could he get away from his wife so as to return to Providence House? The clue is again in the Gardiners' testimony; both Gardiners and Mrs Dickinson agreed they had gone home at 1.30am, and Georgianna said they undressed before retiring to bed at 2am. It wouldn't take a full thirty minutes to get undressed and go to bed and, as Steward suggests, a visit to the privy before bed would seem likely. The privy was situated at the bottom of the garden; it would make sense that Georgianna went first, followed by William. Time was of paramount importance and upon getting downstairs he took the medicine bottle from the cupboard, emptied the contents and filled the bottle with paraffin before plunging the cork deeply into the neck in haste. He gathered up the previous day's copy of the *East Anglian Daily Times* to use so the fire took hold and quickly walked the 200 yards to Providence House. Upon arriving there he saw that nobody had disturbed the scene and he set to work to light the fire. He folded the paper and put it under her head and went to open the bottle but the cork was jammed in too tight. Seeing the kitchen lamp, he dismantled it to take its contents out. Shaking, he couldn't get to the paraffin inside so he could do nothing but smash the medicine bottle, pour what he could get out as fast as he could, before lighting it and leaving immediately to return home, all within fifteen minutes. It is safe to assume that he got home, went upstairs, before getting into bed and falling asleep, no doubt expecting to wake in the morning to learn of a great fire at Providence House and the tragic death of Rose. But Gardiner had again made a blunder; the amount of paraffin he used was pitiful – a small amount would quickly extinguish because enough hadn't been used and only minimal damage had been done. The fact that the fire hadn't taken caused another problem: he'd left the broken medicine bottle with the family name upon it at the scene. By her own admission, Georgianna had had a bad night, getting up to see the children and taking a drink of brandy twice to help her sleep. This makes it plausible that when she did finally fall asleep at 5am she would have been in a deep sleep when Gardiner awoke and slipped out of bed to start the great fire in the wash house before 7am. This is the suggested time at which he disposed of his work Indian rubber-soled shoes and shirt that were covered in blood.

Stammers had testified to seeing a good blaze at 7am and then seeing Gardiner returning at 7.30am to no doubt make sure the evidence was nothing more than a pile of ash. Once it was destroyed, he could start a normal fire to make the tea. A few other names have come and gone in the history of the case but none of them fitted so well all the circumstances of the crime, and certainly no police effort was ever made to apprehend anyone other than William Gardiner.

Rose Harsent's case remains one of the few in British law where a man was tried for murder but no verdict was returned.

Once Gardiner was released after the decision was made that a third trial would be of little use (given the costs and fact that almost everyone outside the village of Peasenhall thought him innocent due to the press campaigns), it must be remembered that Gardiner was to live out his life as a man who was neither innocent nor guilty in the eyes of anyone who recognised him. Had the judicial system allowed for a majority vote as in today's system in sentencing practices he would have been found guilty with a majority of eleven to one in favour of his execution. One person's bravery in holding out against his fellow jurors, and the judge – who held a very biased view which he passed to the jury – is truly outstanding but his anti-capital punishment views meant that from the very second the trial began there would only be one result – not guilty. He alone saved Gardiner from the scaffold from the onset of the second trial.

The prosecution did rely on purely circumstantial evidence alone of course but the overwhelming pull of this led straight to Gardiner.

The murderer must have been in a relationship with Rose and, as we have seen, there was nobody else that can be associated with Rose other than her ex 'fiancé', who had reportedly called their relationship off the previous year, and the writer of the risque letters, Davis, were never suspected because they were deemed as people of good character. This, of course, could be said of Gardiner himself but it appears as if the police were acting on pure instinct. The previous year's rumour meant that Gardener had been instantly suspected by PC Nunn. The defence would try to claim that Rose was a woman of ill repute but this vain attempt was not successful as it was not the truth. She was a bright and bubbly girl and, whilst she enjoyed the attention of her male admirers in the village, she took it no further and there was no long list of lovers that needed to be sifted through. The only person mentioned near and at her time of death was William Gardiner.

Next we take the handwriting used in Rose's letters. How was it possible that the writing was so similar to Gardiner's? Whilst the writing was clearly disguised, the misplaced capital letters were a big giveaway – a practice that Gardiner used in his correspondence. The person would have needed access to the buff envelopes that were used by the seed drill works and were only available to those in an office position; though these envelopes were easily available, these were the ones that Gardiner, being a site manager and foreman, would have used.

Next are the rubber-soled shoes. The shoes Gardiner owned were of the same pattern as those that had been traced to and from Providence House, yet Gardiner denied ever wearing them on that night. The walk to Providence House and back to Alma Cottage would have taken just a few minutes so this would have been no inconvenience to Gardiner in the sense he would have had to make any diversion as not to be seen as the lightning illuminated the backdrop. The knife used in the attack was said to have been like the one Gardiner owned. As Dr Stevenson noted, it had been recently cleaned with only a small amount of blood on it that Gardiner had claimed had resulted from the knife being used recently to gut and skin a rabbit.

The medicine bottle containing paraffin would have had to come from the Gardiners' household at some point since the label bore the family name, and the murderer knew the bottle contained paraffin. The original medicine had been prescribed to the Gardiner children, meaning that had Mrs Gardiner given medicine to help Rose with her cold that it would virtually have been an amount that would have been of no real use to Rose as it was a dose specifically intended for children. And why, if this explanation is to be believed, would Rose use such a small bottle to store paraffin in? She would surely have stored paraffin in much larger containers as Providence House was large, so plenty of paraffin was required to fill the numerous lamps. It is plausible that Rose had been using the small bottle to store paraffin in to keep her lamp topped up but it seems an odd time of night to refill it – surely she would have filled the bottle (or lamp) up earlier in the day, rather than bring it downstairs with the intention of filling it up in the kitchen at that time? It would make much more sense that Gardiner had a premeditated plan to use the paraffin in the bottle that had his family name on to start a fire to burn away any evidence of his wrongdoing (including the bottle itself); he alone would have the necessary access to the bottle within his home.

The request written in the assignation note was for a candle to be placed in the attic window of Rose's room at 10pm that night. The author of the note would have needed to be in such a position to see if the request had been followed through. Gardiner happened to be in a position to observe the window at Providence House at that very time as he was watching the storm gather pace and spoke with Harry Burgess at that time. What are the odds that Gardiner should be at his doorstep at exactly 10pm? The storm began rumbling before this time and intensified greatly after, so why choose exactly 10pm? And, if we assume this was a purely coincidental act, why is it that he walked out from the doorway to a position where the candlelit window of Rose's room was visible from his cottage, as recalled by Harry Burgess who had spoken to Gardiner as he went to the village shop.

Crucially, the murderer would have had to have known that Rose was with child. We will remember that Rose's mother and Mrs Crisp had recently asked her if she was indeed pregnant but Rose had denied this. She was clearly running out of time and was becoming worried that she could no longer hide the obvious from her family and employers. I believe Gardiner was alerted to this by Rose and it quickly became a realization that his world was about to come crashing down around him.

Rumours of the affair were circulating for almost two years before the murder and the scandal had led to the enquiry at the Methodist chapel in May 1901. Wright and Skinner never wavered in their statements, despite the enormous pressure put upon them at the enquiry and then later under cross-examination at the trials. Surely if it was a joke they would have backed down once it became a legal matter and nothing more would be said but they didn't, so were they telling the truth all along?

Henry Rouse spoke to Gardiner after seeing him behaving improperly with Rose in the chapel in late February 1902 and Gardiner promised he would amend his ways. He sent a letter to Gardiner (written by his wife and unsigned) which advised Gardiner to correct his conduct within the chapel. Rouse was subjected to a horrendous attempt by the defence to blacken his character but he, like Wright and Skinner, stuck to his story of events despite originally being on Gardiner's side at the enquiry. Why should he do that if he hadn't seen what he claimed to see? He had nothing to gain from lying about Gardiner and he was not a malicious man; a busybody perhaps, but not malicious.

The letters Gardiner wrote to Rose regarding the rumours are strange in that they were written directly in an attempt to show his innocence; it was almost as if was creating his own alibi. This should have alerted her father or mother to the upcoming events because although Rose was living away from home she was very close to her mother, father and brother. Gardiner's writing to Rose alerted her to his impending actions and acted as a way for them both to get their stories straight before they would be quizzed by the representatives of the chapel and people of Peasenhall. Rose would have been already well informed that the village knew there was an affair going on.

His reason to meet with Rose at the chapel that evening was also poorly thought out. His excuse was that his horse had not eaten up after returning from a trip and that as he was responsible for the company horses he thought he best go back to see if it was well otherwise he would need to call a vet. This is possible, of course, but the fact that this occurred exactly as Rose was having trouble with the chapel door (no reports were recently made of the door sticking) especially given what purportedly followed, was surely not a coincidence.

Stammers attested to Gardiner lighting a great fire at 7.30am on the Sunday morning and thought this was odd behaviour, though Gardiner said it was later than that and the fire was lit to heat the water in the kettle to make a cup of tea. Again, Stammers had no reason to lie; he had no malice towards the Gardiners.

Gardiner was never able to give answers that cleared him from any guilt even though he had months to prepare for the questioning he received at court. It was obviously far easier to convince the church elders of his story because of his position within it and also a question of 'you should believe me rather than two people who are not as us', but when it came to judicial questioning he had no sway over the proceedings, it was an equal playing field and he should have prepared for his answers to questioning far more thoroughly than he did. That said, his legal counsel should also have prepped him for questioning also. He could not do anything more than deny all lines of questioning put to him.

The Peasenhall murder has divided the local community for 120 years. It was a cold and barbaric murder and contained all of the ingredients for a great crime novel. William Gardiner quite literally got away with murder.

Rose Annie Harsent was buried in the local cemetery with just a wooden cross marking her grave. There was great public sympathy for the young girl and a fund was started to raise money to provide her with a gravestone. In 1904 it was completed and put in place and reads as follows:

> In affectionate remembrance of ROSE ANNIE HARSENT
> Whose life was cruelly taken on the 1st June
> 1902 in her 23rd year.
> A light is from our household gone.
> A voice we loved is stilled.
> A place is vacant in our home.
> That never can be filled.

Appendix

List of Names, Who They Were, and Their Relation to the Case

Rose Harsent	Murder victim
William Harsent	Rose's father
Mr And Mrs Crisp	Rose's employers
William Gardiner	The accused
Georgianna Gardiner	The accused's wife
Fred Davis	Writer of letters to Rose
Bob Kerridge	Rose's fiance
Revd. Ernest Cooke	Peasenhall vicar
Dr Lay	Doctor of the village
Herbert Stammers	Witness of the fire at the washhouse
PC Nunn	Policeman of the village
Harry Burgess	Bricklayer and a witness
Mrs Amelia Pepper	Neighbour to Gardiner
Mrs Dickinson	Neighbour to Gardiner
Revd John Guy	Part of the Chapel Sibton Inquiry
Harry Harsent	Rose's brother and a messenger boy
Henry Rouse	Preacher
Alfonso Skinner	Doctor's Chapel eavesdropper
William Wright	Doctor's Chapel eavesdropper
Frederick Brewer	The postman
Sir William Grantham	The judge
Ernest Wild	Lawyer for the defence

Henry Dickens	Lawyer for the prosecution
Thomas Gurrin	Handwriting expert
Dr. Ryder Richardson	The doctor
James Morris	The gamekeeper
George Staunton	Superintendent
James Crisp	Cobbler
Mr Arthur Leighton	The solicitor
Charles Larkin	Handwriting expert
George Andrews	Superintendent
Henry Berry	Inspector

Index

Edwards, Evan, 54–5, 71
Elliston, 67

Felixstowe, 49, 54

Gardiner, Ada Jane, 1
Gardiner, Anna Maria, 1
Gardiner, Bertie George, 3, 48, 85
Gardiner, Caroline, 1
Gardiner, Daisy May, 3, 11
Gardiner, Ernest William,
Gardiner, Ettie May, 2, 75
Gardiner, Georgianna, 2–3, 20,
    27–8, 31, 37, 41, 55–6, 67,
    71–3, 75, 77–81, 87–9
Gardiner, William George, *passim*
Goddard, Abraham, 15, 49
Gooch, Mr, 59
Grantham, Justice Sir William, 39,
    43, 52–3, 62, 68
Green, Mr, 75
Grey, Hon John De, 39
Gurrin, Thomas, 36–7, 46, 66
Guy, Reverend John, 13, 15–16,
    43, 49, 69

Halesworth, 14–15, 24–6, 61
    Magistrates, 59
    Petty Sessions, 82
    Police Station, 31
Harsent, Harry, 10, 34–5, 44,
    60, 76

Harsent, Mr William, 21–2, 30, 46,
    60–1, 76, 85
Harsent, Rose Anne, 3–5,
    7–14, 16–17, 20–8, 30–7,
    39–40, 42–5, 47, 51–3,
    55–8, 60–5, 67–8, 73,
    78–94
Home Office, 24, 37
Hunt, Frances Lizzie, 81
Hunt, Thomas, 45
Hurren, Christianna, 75–6

Ipswich, 27, 37, 54, 56, 61, 65,
    71, 73
    Assize, 54
    Jail, 31
    Shire Hall, 39

Jackson, Harry, 65

Kelsale, 27
Kerridge, Bob, 4, 11, 81

Lambert, Arthur, 83
Lawrence, Justice, 57–9, 64, 68
Lay, Dr, 22–5, 28, 30–2, 34, 36,
    40, 52, 57, 64, 88
Leighton, Arthur Sadler, 31–32,
    34–7, 40, 56, 60, 72–3
Leiston, 27, 86
Levett-Scrivener, Captain,
    29, 35